THE LUCENT LIBRARY OF SCIENCE AND TECHNOLOGY

Telescopes

by James Barter

LUCENT BOOKS

An imprint of Thomson Gale, a part of The Thomson Corporation

THOMSON

GALE

Detroit • New York • San Francisco • San Diego • New Haven, Conn. • Waterville, Maine • London • Munich

THOMSON

GALE

© 2005 Thomson Gale, a part of The Thomson Corporation.

For more information, contact
Lucent Books
27500 Drake Rd.
Farmington Hills, MI 48331-3535
Or you can visit our Internet site at http://www.gale.com

LIBRARY OF CONGRESS CATALOGING-IN-PUBLICATION DATA

Barter, James, 1946–
  Telescopes / by James Barter.
     p. cm. — Lucent library of science and technology)
  Includes bibliographical references and index.
  ISBN 1-59018-568-4 (hardcover : alk. paper)
  1. Telescopes—Juvenile literature. I. Title. II. Series.
QB88.B38 2004
522'.2—dc22   2004013442

Table of Contents

Foreword

"The world has changed far more in the past 100 years than in any other century in history. The reason is not political or economic, but technological—technologies that flowed directly from advances in basic science."

— Stephen Hawking, "A Brief History of Relativity," *Time,* 2000

The twentieth-century scientific and technological revolution that British physicist Stephen Hawking describes in the above quote has transformed virtually every aspect of human life at an unprecedented pace. Inventions unimaginable a century ago have not only become commonplace but are now considered necessities of daily life. As science historian James Burke writes, "We live surrounded by objects and systems that we take for granted, but which profoundly affect the way we behave, think, work, play, and in general conduct our lives."

For example, in just one hundred years, transportation systems have dramatically changed. In 1900 the first gasoline-powered motorcar had just been introduced, and only 144 miles of U.S. roads were hard-surfaced. Horse-drawn trolleys still filled the streets of American cities. The airplane had yet to be invented. Today 217 million vehicles speed along 4 million miles of U.S. roads. Humans have flown to the moon and commercial aircraft are capable of transporting passengers across the Atlantic Ocean in less than three hours.

The transformation of communications has been just as dramatic. In 1900 most Americans lived and worked on farms without electricity or mail delivery. Few people had ever heard a radio or spoken on a telephone. A hundred years later, 98 percent of American homes have telephones and televisions and more than 50 percent have personal computers. Some families even have more than one television and computer, and cell phones are now commonplace, even among the young. Data beamed from communication satellites routinely predict global weather conditions and fiber-optic cable, e-mail, and the Internet have made worldwide telecommunication instantaneous.

Perhaps the most striking measure of scientific and technological change can be seen in medicine and public health. At the beginning of the twentieth century, the average American life span was forty-seven years. By the end of the century the average life span was approaching eighty years, thanks to advances in medicine including the development of vaccines and antibiotics, the discovery of powerful diagnostic tools such as X rays, the life-saving technology of cardiac and neonatal care, and improvements in nutrition and the control of infectious disease.

Rapid change is likely to continue throughout the twenty-first century as science reveals more about physical and biological processes such as global warming, viral replication, and electrical conductivity, and as people apply that new knowledge to personal decisions and government policy. Already, for example, an international treaty calls for immediate reductions in industrial and automobile emissions in response to studies that show a potentially dangerous rise in global temperatures is caused by human activity. Taking an active role in determining the direction of future changes depends on education; people must understand the possible uses of scientific research and the effects of the technology that surrounds them.

The Lucent Books Library of Science and Technology profiles key innovations and discoveries that have transformed the modern world. Each title strives to make a complex scientific discovery, technology, or phenomenon understandable and relevant to the reader. Because scientific discovery is rarely straightforward, each title explains the dead ends, fortunate accidents, and basic scientific methods by which the research into the subject proceeded. And every book examines the practical applications of an invention, branch of science, or scientific principle in industry, public health, and personal life, as well as potential future uses and effects based on ongoing research. Fully documented quotations, annotated bibliographies that include both print and electronic sources, glossaries, indexes, and technical illustrations are among the supplemental features designed to point researchers to further exploration of the subject.

Introduction

Tools to Answer Cosmic Questions

Astronomical observation has its roots in antiquity. Ever since the citizens of ancient Babylonia, China, Egypt, and Greece designed crude wood tools to measure the movement of the stars and planets across the heavens, humankind has been improving those primitive implements to investigate the cosmos and attempt to understand its workings.

Those early astronomical tools, like all tools, were extensions of people's interest to know more—in this case to know more about Earth's celestial movement and the moon's rotation around Earth, and to understand the mechanics of the solar system. Using tools called quadrants and astrolabes, early astronomers answered questions about the regular movement of planets and the distance from Earth to the moon and sun. These devices also aided explorers such as Christopher Columbus and Ferdinand Magellan by determining the earthly position of their ships across the uncharted seas.

As astronomy gradually developed into a science that observes and describes the universe, better astronomical tools replaced older ones. Missing from the astronomer's tool chest for thousands of years, however, was some sort of device capable of improving astronomers' ability to see the stars and planets—one that would allow them to investigate with greater

Modern observatories like this one rely on extremely powerful telescopes to record data from the deepest reaches of space.

precision the great expanse of the universe and to understand its clocklike movements.

When that missing tool, the telescope, finally emerged just four hundred years ago, astronomy shifted gears from an archaic pseudoscience dependent on unaided eyes to understand the universe to a modern technological science reliant on the latest high-tech advances. In the early years of modern astronomy, telescopes answered increasingly complex questions about Earth's rotation around the sun, the size of the solar system and its number of planets, and how many stars are in Earth's galaxy, the Milky Way.

It is not surprising that today, with hundreds of telescopes scattered across the earth and dozens more orbiting in space, they remain the grandest of astronomical tools and the most formidable extension of people's quest to raise questions never imagined by earlier civilizations: How old is the universe, how did it begin, how big is it, and will it last forever?

As long as questions about the cosmos remain unanswered, scientists will improve their telescopes to try and answer them. As astronomer Robert Lin at the University of California's Berkeley campus reminds people, "Astronomy is not a hands-on science. We can't go into deep space to study stars and galaxies; we must rely on our tools."[1] For this reason, twenty-first-century astronomers continue to astound the public by inventing increasingly exotic telescopes, assisted by computer technology, that peer ever deeper into the mysteries of the universe.

Chapter 1

The First Telescope

Magnification, the seminal feature of telescopes, was known as far back as A.D. 1000. A glass sphere called a reading stone was laid on top of the material to be read, magnifying the letters. Salvino D'Armate, an Italian, is credited with inventing the first wearable eyeglasses around 1284, and by the early 1400s eyeglass makers flourished throughout Europe. At that time, the basic similarity between reading lenses and telescopes had not yet been understood. The first generation of astronomers to peer great distances through small, primitive telescopes, and understand that their hands held the key to understanding the cosmos, would not arrive for another two hundred years. Until then, the small, blurry, distant specks in the night sky would remain nothing more than that, even though thinkers for thousands of years had suspected there was more to them than met the eye.

Lenses and Cylinders

With the exception of primitive eyeglasses, the telescope was the first optical instrument constructed, yet its origin is surrounded by controversy. The most likely story places its invention around 1600 in the shop of an obscure Dutch eyeglass maker named Hans Lippershey. According to an often-repeated story, Lippershey's apprentice was playing with two glass lenses that he had shaped and polished for spectacles. By holding one lens close to one eye and the other at arm's length, he inadvertently peered through them in the direction of a distant church steeple. Initially everything was a blur, but the apprentice fiddled with the lenses, changing the distance between them by moving his arm until the image of the church steeple miraculously snapped into focus. Stunned by the sudden clarity of the steeple, the young man stumbled backward by the shock of suddenly seeing it closer than it had been without the lenses. Calling excitedly to his master, the apprentice handed the two lenses to Lippershey, who looked for himself and immediately recognized the significance of the discovery.

Hans Lippershey holds one lens in front of another to magnify a distant object. By mounting two lenses in a wooden tube, Lippershey created the first telescope.

Unable to sleep that night because of his excitement, Lippershey began building a wooden tube to house the two lenses. Three days later, when he mounted the two lenses about two feet apart inside the tube, he created the first telescope, an instrument that he named a "looker."

In 1608, following years of experimentation with improved lenses, tube lengths, and the spacing of the two lenses within the tube, Lippershey sold his looker to the Dutch army. The army's interest was to use the device to spot and estimate the size of an advancing enemy army miles before the enemy spotted the Dutch. News of the invention spread rapidly and other inventors made them. That same year the French ambassador to the Netherlands obtained one for the amusement of King Henry IV, and within the next year, lookers under the name of "Dutch trunks," "perspectives," and "cylinders" were being sold in fashionable shops in Paris, London, and Heidelberg for hunters and sailors.

Word of the magical invention spread south to Venice, Italy. There, an unidentified stranger attempted to sell a looker to a politician, who referred the matter to the city's scientific adviser, Paolo Sarpi. Sarpi carefully examined it and questioned the stranger about its workings. But when the stranger mysteriously departed the city with his instrument, Sarpi went to see Galileo Galilei, the city's most respected instrument maker. Galileo listened intently to the description of the instrument that could magnify distant buildings, and based on what Sarpi had told him, Galileo set out in his workshop to build one.

Galileo Galilei Looks to the Heavens

By 1609, Galileo had constructed several lookers based on several of Lippershey's models and the description he had received from Sarpi. Nothing Galileo had accomplished at this point was particularly noteworthy; many other scientists had become intrigued with the practical application of lookers as a tool for the mili-

Galileo's First Ideas About Telescopes

Galileo is correctly credited with the first use of the telescope for viewing objects in the heavens, but letters between him and friends suggest that he first had other, more pragmatic applications for the telescope. He believed that he could make money selling his telescopes to wealthy Italian princes so that they could use them for military purposes. In Zdenek Kopal's book *Telescopes in Space*, the author provides two such letters, the first dating from 1609 and the second from 1610.

One letter to the Doge of Venice suggests that telescopes would be best suited as instruments of war:

> The power of my cannocchiale [telescope] to show distant objects as clearly as if they were near should give us an inestimable advantage in any military action on land or sea. At sea, we shall be able to spot their flags two hours before they can see us; and when we have established the number and type of the enemy craft, we shall be able to decide whether to pursue and engage him in battle, or take flight. Similarly, on land it should be possible from elevated positions to observe the enemy camps and their fortifications.

Less than a year later, when Galileo was seeking employment as a mathematician at the palace of the Grand Duke of Tuscany in the city of Florence, he wrote about his telescope: "I have many and most admirable devices; but they could only be put to work by princes because it is they who are able to carry on wars, build and defend fortresses, and for their regal sport make most splendid expenditures."

Pictured is a reconstruction of Galileo's telescope. Initially, Galileo believed the telescope would best serve as an instrument of war.

tary, sailors at sea, and long-distance signaling. Galileo, however, would soon liberate these early telescopes from their limited terrestrial applications.

In early 1610, while sitting at his outside worktable in the evening, Galileo did something far more intriguing and prophetic with his telescope than simply taking another look at a distant church spire or sailing ship. He tilted one of his many lookers skyward and pulled up a chair for a more comfortable view. Staring into space, Galileo moved the cylinder around until he began spotting distant objects in the solar system. Stunned by the unexpected density of stars and planets, Galileo recorded the first fundamental discoveries about the solar system that could not be noted with the naked eye. Pointing the looker at the moon, he was dumbfounded to discover its surface texture

Galileo and the Church

Galileo's many observations of the solar system led the famous mathematician and astronomer to conclude that the planets revolved around the sun. However, he was not the first to propose such an idea. In 1514, the Polish mathematician Nicolaus Copernicus published a book titled *Little Commentary* in which he set forth several principles, which he called axioms, concerning the solar system. One of the axioms stated that Earth was not the center of the universe, and a second argued that all the planets including Earth were in motion around the center of the universe near the sun.

Although Galileo's acceptance of the Copernican view of the solar system was not revolutionary, it nonetheless attracted the attention of the Catholic Church. Church authorities had cited passages from the Bible that they believed indicated that God had made Earth the center of the universe, with all other bodies revolving around it. As word spread about Galileo's contradiction of church doctrine, Pope Urban VIII summoned him to Rome to express his displeasure.

In 1616, Pope Urban ordered Galileo to admit he had erred in supporting the Copernican theory that Earth revolves around the sun. Galileo's refusal to recant created friction between Europe's most famous scientist and the pope. Following years of charges and countercharges, in 1633 Galileo was tried by a church court and found guilty of continuing to promote his theory. He was placed under arrest, yet continued writing while living out the rest of his life under papal confinement.

of mountains and plains pocked with deep craters. Rotating it toward Jupiter he made the discovery that the distant planet had four moons. Of even greater significance, Galileo eventually provided the first primitive mapping of the major stars of Earth's galaxy, the Milky Way. Based on nothing more than brightness, he mapped the largest stars into seven concentric circles that he called "magnitudes." Magnitude 1, the innermost circle, contained the stars nearest to Earth, while magnitude 7 contained those farthest away. When he was done with this huge task, one evening he wrote in his journal:

> You will behold through the looker a host of other stars, which escape the unassisted sight, so numerous as to be beyond belief. Stars of the seventh magnitude appear with the aid of the looker larger and brighter than stars of the second magnitude seen with the unassisted sight.[2]

Galileo named his most recently built looker "Old Discoverer" and commented in letters to his friends that it was his best of more than one hundred previous models. Barely three feet long and containing two magnifying lenses, each one inch in diameter, it was capable of magnifying objects twenty-eight times their actual size. The light from distant stars, he explained, was refracted, or bent, as it struck the two lenses magnifying it. Old Discoverer was therefore an early refracting telescope. The historic instrument is now on display at the Institute and Museum of the History of Science in Florence, Italy.

In March 1610, Galileo published a description of his night sky observations titled *Sidereus Nuncius*, Latin for *The Starry Messenger*. This twenty-four-page book excited scientific thinkers with detailed descriptions of the heavens yet unseen by other scientists. Galileo revealed to his readers the distant scatter of night light to be millions upon millions of stars and colorful swirls of what appeared to be dust (which astronomers now know to be dense gases). In a more general and controversial statement, Galileo challenged the Catholic Church's teachings that Earth was the center of the universe. Agreeing with his predecessor Nicolaus Copernicus, Galileo boldly argued that Earth orbited the sun along with the other planets.

Galileo was delighted with his discoveries but disturbed by the sharp criticism he received from the church. Most church leaders believed his observations to be preposterous and blasphemous because they contradicted the church's contention that Earth was the center of the universe—a belief based on the importance of humankind in scripture. Catholic authorities told Galileo that his looker did nothing more than create optical illusions. The church insisted that the images he and other scientists saw could not be trusted.

On the night of April 14, 1611, to demonstrate their support for Galileo's controversial discoveries, scientists outside Rome held a banquet in Galileo's honor. Galileo let them peer through Old Discoverer. An unidentified Greek poet happened to be present who proposed that the refracting looker be given the name *telescope*, a Greek word meaning "to see into the distance."

Galileo's dispute with theologians was ongoing and placed him in conflict with them for the remainder of his life. Still, Galileo gave telescopes and astronomy the first major scientific boost. The contemporary astronomer N.M. Swerdlow said of Galileo's astronomical discoveries: "In about two months, December and January [1609–1610], he made more discoveries with his telescope that changed the world than anyone has ever made before or since."[3] The European astronomers who followed Galileo were eager to improve upon his findings and test the abilities of telescopes to explore the universe more thoroughly.

A Surge of Refracting Telescopes

Following Lippershey and Galileo, the objective of the next generation of telescope builders was twofold: To increase the light-collecting capability of telescopes and to improve their resolution, or sharpness of focus. In order to achieve these objectives, a major problem had to be resolved. Glass lenses, which had to be polished to form a slight concavity or curvature, caused incoming light to refract, or bend, just as a stick inserted halfway in water appears to bend below the surface. The amount of refraction varied depending upon the different wavelengths of entering light. Each wavelength corresponds to a different color; red has the longest wavelength and violet has the shortest. This means that the focus point for each wavelength, or color, lies at a different distance from the lens. As a result, all the light coming down an early telescope

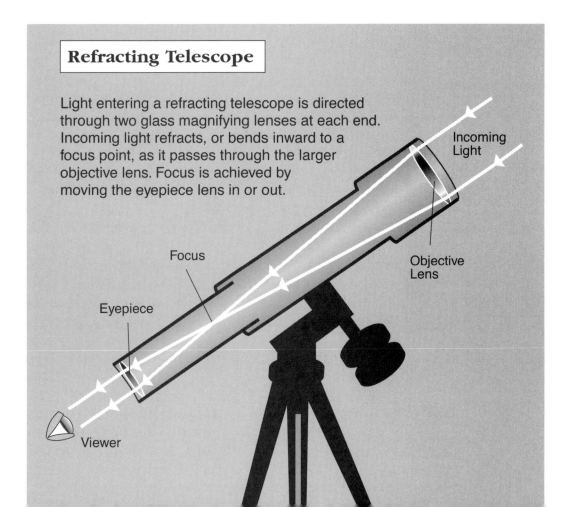

Refracting Telescope

Light entering a refracting telescope is directed through two glass magnifying lenses at each end. Incoming light refracts, or bends inward to a focus point, as it passes through the larger objective lens. Focus is achieved by moving the eyepiece lens in or out.

Incoming Light

Focus

Objective Lens

Eyepiece

Viewer

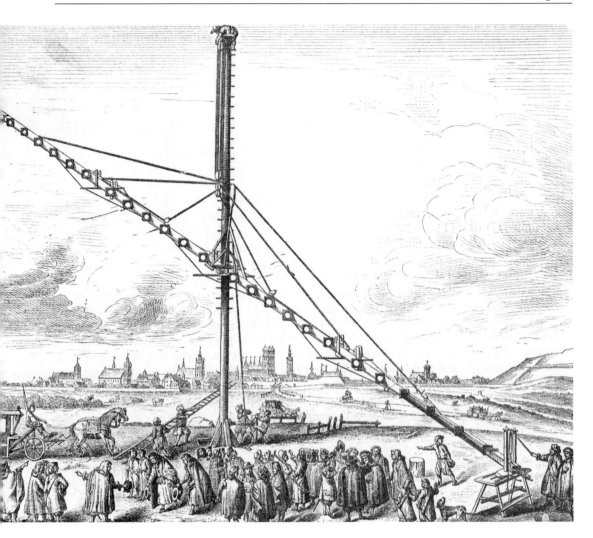

Polish astronomer Hevelius built this telescope that measured 158 feet in length. Although the telescope had great magnifying power, its size made the instrument unwieldy.

tube could not be focused at a single point for the observer's eye. An astronomer looking at a distant object saw the object surrounded by what appeared to be a halo of color similar to a circular rainbow. This distracting phenomenon is known to astronomers as chromatic aberration, although its cause was originally unknown.

What astronomers did know from trial and error was that the easiest way to reduce chromatic aberration was to flatten the lenses while increasing the space between them, called the focal length. With flatter lenses, all wavelengths of light would focus better at the eye of the observer, and as the focal length increased, so did magnification.

The last of these two design changes touched off a competition to see who could build the longest refracting telescope. Although the lenses did not grow much in size (about six to eight inches in diameter), the barrel lengthened to enormous proportions. An astronomer by the name of Hevelius of Danzig provided detailed mappings of the moon using a telescope with an astonishing focal length of 158 feet. The problem with such long, narrow, and unwieldy contrivances was twofold. First, transporting the long, narrow tubes was a major feat, and second, once a location was chosen, setting the barrel sections in a perfectly straight line was almost impossible.

In 1663, recognizing that the problem of chromatic aberration was not being completely eliminated by longer and longer refracting telescopes, the Scottish mathematician James Gregory published *Optica Promota*, in which he described the first practical reflecting telescope (now known as the Gregorian telescope). Rather than using lenses that refract light, his revolutionary contribution was to describe mathematically the capture of light by a mirror that reflected the light to an astronomer's eyepiece. The use of mirrors instead of glass lenses to capture and focus light meant that the tube of the Gregorian telescope could be shorter but of larger diameter than refractor telescopes. Unfortunately, Gregory never built his reflector telescope; that task would fall to the English mathematician Isaac Newton.

Isaac Newton's Innovation

In 1670, Isaac Newton was a young mathematician studying the mathematics and physics of optics at Cambridge University in England. During his research, he reached the conclusion that visible sunlight was not as simple an entity as his predecessors had supposed.

Every scientist since Aristotle had believed that sunlight was a simple, pure phenomenon, but the chromatic aberration in telescope lenses convinced Newton that sunlight required further investigation.

As an experiment to determine whether sunlight was a single entity or something more complicated, Newton made a glass prism and placed it on a table in his Cambridge apartment. He then drilled a small hole in the window shutter and closed the shutter to darken the room except for the single beam of sunlight passing through the tiny hole. He then positioned the prism on the table so that a beam of light would pass through the prism and project on the opposite wall. Newton theorized that if sunlight is a composite of many colors, he would see a smear of color on the wall. As he slid the prism into the path of the ray of light and turned to see the result, his answer appeared in a blaze of individual colors stretched out on the wall.

Dazzled by what he had discovered, Newton received credit for the revolutionary discovery that sunlight is a mixture of many different wavelengths that are refracted at slightly different angles and that each different wavelength produces a different spectral color. Observing the colorful spectrum of light on the wall, Newton correctly concluded that at the far left of the spectrum, red had the longest wavelength, followed by orange, yellow, green, blue, indigo, and, shortest at the far right, violet. Newton recognized that this was the very same arrangement of colors seen in the spectrum of rainbows and in chromatic aberration.

Now knowing that light was refracted into the spectrum, Newton erroneously concluded that telescopes using refracting lenses would always suffer chromatic aberration. He could think of no solution to correct it. As a result, Newton constructed a new type of telescope based on Gregory's *Optica Promota* that could magnify and focus light by reflecting it rather than refracting it.

Reflection Rather than Refraction

Newton drew up his first design in 1670 but did not receive scientific acclaim for it until he published his ideas more fully in 1700 in his treatise *Opticks*. What made Newton's telescope unique to seventeenth-century astronomers was his abandonment of a glass lens through which light passed to focus and form an image,

Isaac Newton invented this telescope that magnified and focused light using mirrors. Also pictured is a manuscript page with Newton's drawing of the telescope.

in favor of a concave mirror off of which light reflected to focus and form an image.

Newton, following Gregory's design, demonstrated that a concave mirror focuses all wavelengths of sunlight at the same point, thereby avoiding the troublesome chromatic aberration produced by refracting telescopes. Newton's telescope, now on display at the Royal Society in London, was just 12 inches long with a primary mirror 1.5 inches in diameter. Using mirrors solved the problem of excessively long, unwieldy refracting tubes. In addition, the magnification power of Newton's reflective mirror reached 38, making Newton's instrument decidedly more powerful than Galileo's refracting telescope.

Newton's reflecting telescope worked in an entirely new way. Light from space was collected by the primary concave mirror and then reflected and focused back on a smaller secondary concave mirror. This secondary mirror was inclined at a forty-five-degree angle to the primary mirror to reflect a second time the focused light to an eyepiece on the side of the telescope barrel, where an astronomer could view the image. By all historical accounts, Newton was far more fascinated by the mathematics and mechanics of telescopes than he was by looking through them into space. Few of his letters discuss observations on the night sky, yet hundreds discuss building telescopes and perfecting mirrors. All mirrors at this time were fabricated from a metal alloy consisting of three parts copper, one part tin, and one part arsenic. The arsenic was added to impart the highest reflective coating possible. Hours of shaping and then polishing were required. In 1704, Newton wrote about polishing a primary mirror:

> I ground the object metal with a brisk motion for three or four minutes of time with pitch [resin], leaning hard upon it. Then I placed fresh putty [polishing grit] and ground it again until it had done making a noise [grinding sound], and this

work I repeated until the metal was polished, grinding it the last time with all my strength and frequently breathing upon the pitch, to keep it moist without laying on any more putty.[4]

Contemporary optical engineers estimate that Newton's mirrors reflected little more than 15 percent of the light entering the telescope tube. Nonetheless, his telescope design was a monumental and historic improvement over refracting telescopes. His reflecting telescope not only avoided the problem of chromatic aberration but also focused more accurately and was easily transportable. Best of all, it could see more distant objects than Hevelius's cumbersome contraption.

The new reflecting telescope, however, was not without its problems. Having the eyepiece on the side of the barrel was inconvenient for astronomers, and the secondary mirror tilted at its forty-five-degree angle caused some degradation of incoming light. In 1672, the Frenchman Guillaume Cassegrain was reviewing Newton's telescope design and devised a remedy to the tilted secondary mirror and to the side-mounted eyepiece. His solution, which was named after him, continues to be incorporated into the designs of modern reflector telescopes. Cassegrain proposed three significant design changes. First, the secondary mirror should be convex rather than concave. Second, the secondary mirror should be set parallel (face to face) to the primary mirror rather than at a forty-five-degree angle. And third, and most important of all, a small hole should be drilled in the very center of the primary mirror to allow the light ray, as reflected by the secondary mirror, to pass through and reach an astronomer viewing from the tail end of the barrel.

With these revolutionary enhancements, entering light is first captured by the primary mirror and focused back on the smaller secondary mirror, which in turn focuses it back through the small center hole in the primary mirror on its way to the astronomer's eye.

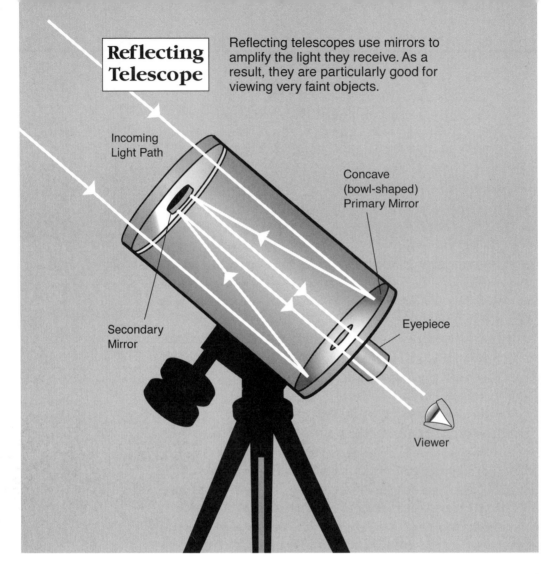

Reflecting Telescope

Reflecting telescopes use mirrors to amplify the light they receive. As a result, they are particularly good for viewing very faint objects.

Incoming Light Path

Concave (bowl-shaped) Primary Mirror

Secondary Mirror

Eyepiece

Viewer

Using this design, there is less degradation of light and the observer can more handily point the telescope in the direction of observation.

Solving the Problem of Chromatic Aberration

Design improvements by Newton and Cassegrain made reflecting telescopes far more valuable to astronomers than refracting telescopes, but they continued to be plagued by poor-quality metal mirrors. Constantly in need of polishing, metal mirrors quickly distorted and corroded. Seventeenth-century astronomers found themselves spending far too much time grinding and polishing instead of stargazing.

Some time during the mid-1730s, amateur astronomers frustrated by metal mirrors attacked the problem of chromatic aberration in spite of Newton's pronouncement that no solution was possible. By experimenting with a variety of different types of glass lenses, the Englishman Chester Moor Hall stumbled on a solution. Being an amateur, he contracted with optician George Bass to make two 2.5-inch lenses, one made of crown glass (exceptionally hard and clear with low refraction) and the other a concave lens of flint glass (soft and heavy with high refraction). When Bass combined the two, he discovered that they eliminated chromatic aberration. This combination of lenses was called an achromatic lens.

Failing to understand the significance of his discovery, Bass neglected to notify Hall. Then, twenty years later, in the mid-1750s, Bass contacted John Dollond about the achromatic lens. John's son, Peter, saw a commercial application for the lens and applied for a patent. When Hall found out about it, he sued in court but lost because, although he had conceived the idea, he had failed to bring it to fruition. By 1780, hundreds of astronomers snapped up Dollond's lenses, mounted them to refracting telescopes only a few feet long, and saw the stars and planets more clearly than ever.

Such an improved refracting telescope did not end the refractor versus reflector debate and competition. What it did resolve, however, as the eighteenth century came to a close, was that telescopes were destined to become larger.

Chapter 2

The Era of the Giants

During the later part of the eighteenth century, while European astronomers debated the merits and deficiencies of both refracting and reflecting telescopes, the Englishman William Herschel recognized that regardless of the type of telescope, the larger the lens or mirror, the better the image created. Herschel's conclusion prompted a race among astronomers to build giant telescopes, a competition that continues to this day.

In 1774, at the relatively late age of thirty-five, Herschel abandoned the life of a professional musician to focus on constructing telescopes and observing the heavens. After making inquiries about purchasing a five- or six-foot-long reflector telescope, only to learn that no instrument that size had ever been built, Herschel sat down to cast and polish several nine-inch mirrors for a ten-foot-long Gregorian telescope of his own design. Herschel's sister Caroline, who shared Herschel's interests, wrote that on one occasion, "in order to finish a mirror, he had not taken his hands from it for sixteen hours."[5] Herschel's hard work had its reward. In 1776, he wrote in his journal that he had spent the night looking at "Saturn's ring and two belts in great perfection."[6] Herschel was delighted to boast that his instrument, more powerful than any previous telescope, achieved a magnification power of 240. Using such a telescope in March 1781, Herschel was the first to see the planet Uranus, the fifth known planet of the solar system, and to map and identify over two thousand star clusters and nebulae, which are large clouds of interstellar dust and gas created by cosmic explosions.

The First Observatory

In 1786, Herschel's quest to make more discoveries motivated him to buy a larger house and grounds to accommodate an unprecedented forty-four reflector telescope with a forty-eight-inch primary mirror. A telescope of this magnitude would exceed the weight and size of earlier models that could be manually tilted and rotated to peer into the night sky. Such a herculean task would now require a complex structure to support and aim an iron tube of several hundred pounds to house the primary and secondary mirrors. Herschel also needed to build a structure to house all of the instrumentation required to observe the heavens.

Herschel initially hired forty workmen to pour a concrete foundation on which the telescope and its supporting structure could rotate to any direction in the sky. Next he designed and supervised the construction of the wood frame for the observatory. Although he did not design a roof to protect the telescope from the elements, the observatory required a complex wood structure in the shape of a pyramid to support the telescope's weight. This sixty-foot-tall structure consisted of long primary beams supported by hundreds of diagonal braces to provide sturdy support. Attached to this system of beams and braces were ladders that led to a platform at the elevated end of the telescope where Herschel could make fine adjustments to the telescope and clean it when necessary.

On the interior floor of the observatory, where Herschel would sit and make his observations, he built a small cottage to protect him from the weather. He cut a hole in the roof of the cottage to accommodate

English astronomer William Herschel built this huge reflecting telescope in the late 1700s. A wooden structure was needed to help support and adjust the telescope.

one end of the protruding barrel. When the structure was completed, Herschel went to work on a frame of wood, canvas slings, pulleys, and heavy ropes that would cradle the telescope, allowing him to elevate or lower it for precise aiming toward any cosmic location.

As an adjunct to the observatory, Herschel constructed work sheds where the telescope would be made and later repaired. In one, a crew forged the forty-foot-long iron tube that would house the mirrors. In a second, Herschel cast the world's largest mirror. To improve the quality of the mirror, he experimented with the composition of the metals to achieve more resistance to corrosion. He increased the concentration of copper and arsenic while slightly reducing the tin content. He also experimented with a thin coating of silver for greater reflectivity.

"The Greatest Observer Who Ever Lived"

All of Herschel's efforts paid off. Three years after beginning his observatory, while peering through his forty-eight-inch telescope, he discovered two more of Jupiter's moons, bringing the known total at that time to six. His observations of what had previously been considered indistinguishable globular clusters of light revealed distinct star clusters within the Milky Way. Looking at the constellation of Orion, Herschel expressed his satisfaction with the quality of his big mirror: "The object I viewed was the nebula in the belt of Orion, and I found the figure in the mirror, though far from perfect, better than I had expected. It showed the four small stars in the Nebula and many more. The Nebula was extremely bright."[7]

In 1781 Herschel went on to identify Uranus, the first planet discovered since antiquity, prompting him to say, "I have looked further into space than any human being did before me."[8] During the early nineteenth century, while mapping the Milky Way, he was the first to demonstrate that the entire solar system moves through space. Accomplishing so many things with this one telescope prompted the modern astronomer Patrick Moore to comment, "William Herschel was the first man to give a reasonably correct picture of the shape of our star-system or galaxy; he was the best telescope-maker of his time, and possibly the greatest observer who ever lived."[9]

Herschel's discoveries place him among the pantheon of modern astronomers. Yet, the problems with mirrors continued to plague the science of astronomy. Metals were difficult to grind and even more difficult to keep free of corrosion. Before astronomers would see farther into space and with greater resolution, a solution to these mirror problems was needed.

The First Glass Mirror

At the same time that Herschel was exploring the universe, glassmaking technology was improving. Dozens of household objects such as drinking glasses, flower vases, and elaborately decorated bowls were made using the latest glassblowing and molding techniques. One type in particular, decorative glass bowls with a silver interior film that reflected light onto the bowl's contents, caught the attention of astronomers.

About 1860, seizing on the process of making reflecting glass bowls, the French physicist Jean-Bernard-Léon Foucault achieved notable success when he manufactured a four-inch and then a twelve-inch glass telescope mirror with a silver surface capable of greater reflectivity than the finest polished metal. Since the mirror was made of glass, once it was ground and polished, it would be corrosion-free and would never require further polishing.

Within twenty years, silver-coated glass mirrors became standard throughout Europe. Glassmakers realized that they could heat molten glass, pour it into molds shaped for curved mirrors, impress the initial curve onto the surface, and thereby reduce the amount of grinding. And as glass manufacturing progressed, so did the silvering technique. By 1880 a fifteen-inch glass mirror achieved a 1,200 magnification power, far superior to Herschel's forty-eight-inch metallic mirror. The discovery of the glass mirror was the missing link needed for larger reflecting telescopes, and it sounded the death knell for refracting telescopes.

The Mt. Wilson Sixty Inch

The twentieth century opened with the construction of the largest mirror yet conceived. Measuring sixty inches in diameter, with a thickness of eight inches, and weighing two thousand pounds, the mirror had

The First Astronomical Photograph

For three hundred years telescopes had been used to discover distant celestial bodies, but it was not until the late nineteenth century that they were first used to document their discoveries. On the night of September 30, 1880, American amateur astronomer Henry Draper obtained the first astronomical photograph—a picture of the Great Nebula of Orion.

Draper had experimented with the daguerreotype camera, the first camera invented, one of which he mounted to a telescope eyepiece. With a very slow shutter speed of 104 minutes, the image of the nebula was shot on an eleven-inch achromatic telescope. The resulting photographs were not very impressive, but Draper made further refinements by mounting better-quality cameras on the telescope's eyepiece and adjusting the exposure time.

Other photographic firsts for Draper include the first wide-angle photograph of a comet's tail and the first spectrum of a comet's head in 1881. In addition, Draper obtained many high-quality photographs of the moon, some of which he enlarged to five inches in diameter, a revolutionary improvement over smaller ones.

In the 1880s Henry Draper took detailed photographs of the moon and other celestial bodies with the telescopic camera he invented.

been cast fourteen years earlier by the Saint-Gobain glassworks in France. When completed, it was shipped to Pasadena, California, where the final shaping and polishing were done, and in 1908 the mirror was installed in an observatory atop Mt. Wilson.

The telescope was placed under the supervision of lead astronomer George Ellery Hale, whose multimillionaire father had purchased the mirror for him for the then enormous price of $25,000. Hale's objective for the world's largest telescope was to see more distant objects with greater resolution than ever before.

Hale received accolades for building the sixty-inch telescope, but it was Edwin Hubble, director of the observatory, who gained recognition as one of America's most esteemed astronomers while using this instrument to make revolutionary discoveries about the nature of the Milky Way. Hubble and his colleague Harlow Shapley used the sixty-inch telescope to determine the position of the solar system within the galaxy. They were also the first to measure the size of the Milky Way, estimating it to be about ninety thousand light-years across (one light-year is the distance light travels in one year, roughly 5.9 trillion miles) and containing roughly 200 billion stars. They also determined that the galaxy is in the shape of a spiral, with a bulged central section and radial arms that start in the center and extend outward to form a flat pinwheel shape. They pinpointed the position of the solar system about two-thirds of the way out from the center of one of the arms, named the Orion Arm, and established the arm's thickness to be about three thousand light-years.

As astronomers looked deep into space, many trillions of miles, for the first time, they were astonished by the magnitude of the Milky Way and the vast distances between Earth and its newly discovered intergalactic neighbors. Hubble and Hale were two of several pioneering astronomers to recognize that when they studied distant stars, they were actually peering

George Ellery Hale

George Ellery Hale remains one of the giants of twentieth-century astronomy. He was born in Chicago in 1868, an only child and heir to his family's considerable fortune. Hale developed an interest in astronomy at a young age and benefited from the considerable financial support of his father, who purchased for him several sophisticated telescopes and spectrometers. At the age of twenty-three, Hale had his own private solar astronomical laboratory. By then he had graduated from the Massachusetts Institute of Technology and his scientific reputation was already well established.

Over the years Hale organized three world-class astronomical observatories. In the 1890s he secured funding for the University of Chicago's Yerkes Observatory, which housed the then-largest telescope in the world. Afterward he secured funds for the establishment of a solar observatory on Mt. Wilson in California, of which he became director in 1904 and which long remained the best solar observatory in the world, housing the world's largest telescope of its time. Though he did not live to see the project completed in 1948, Hale was the main force behind the construction of the two-hundred-inch telescope on Mt. Palomar in California. Later in life, suffering from recurrent episodes of depression, Hale resigned as director of the Mt. Wilson Observatory in 1923 and retired from active scientific research. On February 21, 1938, he died in Pasadena, California.

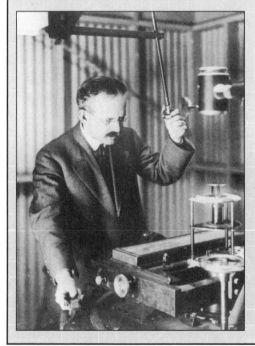

George Ellery Hale established three astronomical observatories that employed state-of-the-art instruments.

back in time to see the stars as they once were, not as they are in the present. This perplexing yet important phenomenon is known to astronomers as "look-back time."

A Look Back in Time

Light from distant stars travels at 186,000 miles per second, and according to the preeminent physicist Albert Einstein, nothing can exceed this speed. This speed limit means that even though light travels extremely fast, it still takes time to travel across the expansive universe. What early twentieth-century astronomers realized as they peered far into space was that the images they were looking at represented objects as they existed in the past, not as they exist in the present.

This perplexing phenomenon leads to the observation that telescopes actually look back in time. They tell astronomers, for example, how planets and stars 1 billion light-years away appeared 1 billion years ago, not as they appear today relative to Earth's time. In many cases, the stars photographed in deep space no longer exist, but astronomers won't know that until one day when they point their telescopes in the direction of a known star, only to discover it is no longer there. Thus, the seemingly simple question, "What is occurring right now on the cluster of stars called the Pleiades?" cannot be answered by an astronomer because it takes their light four hundred years to reach Earth. What astronomers see today when peering at this star cluster is how it existed when Lippershey and Galileo made their early contributions to astronomy.

The success of the sixty-inch telescope peering far back in time spurred scientists to build a much larger telescope capable of seeing even farther back. In 1917, while the sixty-inch telescope was making headlines, Hale and the Carnegie Institution planned to develop a telescope with an even larger mirror. They proposed and received funding for a one-hundred-inch telescope to be housed next to the sixty inch on Mt. Wilson. The new, larger telescope's mirror would be able to capture almost three times as much light as the sixty inch, making it far more effective for exploring the mysteries of the Milky Way and beyond.

Discovering the Expanding Universe

On July 1, 1917, the one-hundred-inch Hooker telescope arrived on Mt. Wilson with great fanfare. It was named in honor of John D. Hooker, a local business-man who provided the funds for the giant mirror in the largest telescope in the world at that time. Saint-Gobain glassworks fabricated the mirror from the same glass used for wine bottles. Holding the world's record as the largest solid plate glass mirror ever cast, the thirteen-inch-thick, nine-thousand-pound mirror

The one-hundred-inch reflecting telescope at the Mt. Wilson observatory offered astronomers their first glimpses of the universe beyond the Milky Way.

made its way up Mt. Wilson to begin laying the foundation for several of the most far-reaching discoveries about the origin of the universe.

When the mirror arrived, engineers in charge of the final polishing were shocked to discover bubbles within the mirror that were created when the blank was poured. The Saint-Gobain facilities were the best in the world, but they did not have the means to melt and pour nine thousand pounds of glass in a single casting. Three pours were required, and that trapped air bubbles between each layer. The bubbles appeared as waves and swirls frozen in place, with some bubbles coming to within a fraction of an inch of the polished surface. Satisfied the surface was not diminished, engineers applied the final reflective coating as astronomers from around the world waited with great anticipation for new astronomical discoveries.

Their wait did not last long. Many astronomers consider that the Hooker telescope provided some of the greatest astronomical views and discoveries of the universe beyond the Milky Way. With this one-hundred-inch telescope, Edwin Hubble reported for the first time the distances and velocities of neighboring galaxies. This demonstrated that these galaxies are separate entities and not small nebulae contained within the Milky Way, as many astronomers had previously believed. Hubble also produced the most dazzling photographs of a seemingly infinite number of stars, spinning galaxies, and other mystifying phenomena that could not be viewed with the smaller sixty-inch mirror.

Hubble's greatest discovery would come in 1929 when he proved that the universe was expanding in all directions at a constant speed, a figure now referred to as "Hubble's constant." Knowing the rate of expansion, he was then able to estimate the age of the universe, placing it between 10 billion and 20 billion years. Combining these two findings meant that when the universe was much younger, it also had to have been much smaller. This conclusion eventually led to the theory, accepted by most astronomers today, that the universe was born at one instant in time in an explosion of energy called "the big bang." At that instant, the universe was a super-dense super-hot speck. Once the big bang occurred, the universe expanded from that point and has been expanding and cooling ever since.

By the end of the 1920s, astronomers were dazzled by the Mt. Wilson discoveries. They lobbied for even larger telescopes if such mind-bending discoveries were to continue. They pondered what might be discovered by building a monster telescope with a two-hundred-inch mirror, creating a reflective surface four times larger than the Hook mirror.

The Mt. Palomar Observatory

In 1930, Hale and the California Institute of Technology (Caltech) were awarded a grant of money by the Rockefeller Foundation to construct a two-hundred-inch telescope. Numerous locations were tested for the atmospheric conditions needed for optimum astronomical observing, and in 1934 Palomar Mountain, sixty miles northeast of San Diego, California, was selected. With part of his $6 million grant, Hale purchased 160 acres of land atop the mountain at an elevation of fifty-six hundred feet.

Finding the money and location for the world's largest telescope was the easy part. Fabricating the mirror would be the biggest headache because no one had ever attempted to create such a large mirror, and the larger the mirror, the greater the likelihood of casting failure.

Difficulties in Constructing the Big Eye

Hale approached the Corning Glass Works with a proposal to build the two-hundred-inch mirror, but after spending $1 million, optical engineers had achieved nothing but cracked blanks as the molten fused quartz glass cooled. Hale then recommended the use of a new

Edwin Hubble sits inside the telescope at the Mt. Palomar observatory. Palomar's two-hundred-inch telescope is able to detect objects as far as 10 billion light-years away.

glass blend called Pyrex that was much less prone to cracking and had fewer distortion problems than those that plagued the one-hundred-inch telescope. On their second attempt using Pyrex, Corning engineers succeeded in casting the twenty-six-inch-thick mirror. After slowly cooling it over eight months, the forty-thousand-pound blank, with only a rough flat surface, was shipped across the country, from New York to Pasadena, on a specially designed railroad car. The telescope project captured the public's imagination, and thousands of people lined the tracks to catch a glimpse of the enormous, crated mirror pass by on a specially constructed freight car at a top speed of twenty-five miles per hour. Guards were posted around the mirror during overnight stops to prevent any tampering that might damage it.

At the end of the fourteen-day trip, Caltech engineers ground the surface of the mirror to the approximate required concavity. Using successively finer polishing grit, the opticians then carefully smoothed the surface, constantly using optical tests to compare it with the desired curvature. When completed, the mirror had lost almost ten thousand pounds of glass. After thirteen years of grinding and polishing, interrupted by World War II, the "Big Eye," as it was named, achieved the desired form.

In 1948, the Big Eye, later named the Hale telescope in honor of its creator, captured "first light" by viewing and photographing distant objects only 1/40,000,000 as bright as the dimmest object visible to the naked eye. Capable of seeing objects billions of light-years more distant than the Hook telescope, the Hale's scope of work over the years was extraordinary.

Accomplishments of the Hale

Operating almost 365 nights a year, the Hale has been a workhorse. It was the first telescope to focus principally on celestial objects far beyond the Milky Way and the range of the one-hundred-inch Hook. Some of these objects that reside as far as 10 billion light-years from Earth, were originally thought to be stars. Hale clearly showed that they were actually "quasi-stellar objects," a term later abbreviated to *quasars*. Quasars are peculiar objects that radiate as much energy per second as a thousand or more galaxies, yet they have a diameter about one-millionth that of galaxy. Astronomers at Mt. Palomar were the first to suggest that quasars are associated with black holes and that they derive their awesome power from large quantities of gas pouring into a nearby black hole so rapidly that the energy output is a thousand times greater than the galaxy itself.

In the late 1950s, most of the evenings for the two-hundred-inch telescope were dedicated to exploring deep space in search of unusual, spectacular galaxies formed within 1 billion years of the big bang. The types of galaxies astronomers were looking for were those demonstrating some sort of cataclysmic event. The cataclysms are often the result of galaxies colliding, a phenomenon that chiefly occurred near the time of the big bang when celestial bodies had yet to fan out into the depths of space. Within a few years, several of these galaxies were located, and the resulting photographs depict massive gaseous explosions and halos of hot debris ejected into space.

Three separate images provided by the Hale telescope show the movement of Sedna, the most distant object yet discovered in our solar system.

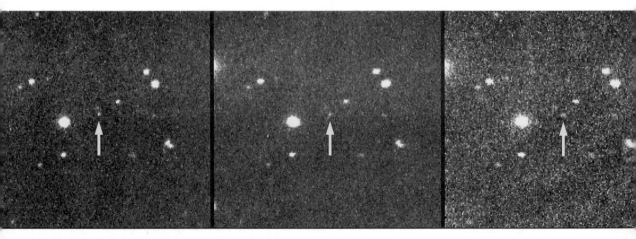

In March 2004, the Hale made a discovery close to home, yet it was just as surprising to astronomers as their discoveries about distant quasars and colliding galaxies. Peering just 8 billion miles from Earth—the distance light travels in just twelve hours—astronomers were stunned to discover a small planet orbiting the sun. Named Sedna, this most recently discovered member of the solar system is three times more distant from the sun than Pluto. Astronomers are currently debating whether Sedna qualifies as the solar system's tenth planet or is simply a lowly planetoid.

For more than 350 years, since Lippershey and Galileo, astronomers steadily improved telescopes capable of capturing light from the most distant recesses of the universe. During that same period, physicists also discovered that there were other forms of light besides the light detectable by the eye. Eventually, some postulated, someone would figure out a way to detect light invisible to the eye.

Chapter 3

Radio Telescopes: Discovering the Invisible Universe

In 1932, while working for Bell Labs in New Jersey, physicist Karl Jansky made a rather unsettling discovery. Jansky's work dealt with the problems of radio and telephone communications, and he had been assigned the task of tracking down the crackling static noises that plagued early overseas telephone reception. Stymied by the source of the interference, Jansky constructed a large but crude antenna system that he could rotate. He then recorded in magnetic tape two well-known kinds of atmospheric static: sharp crashes from local thunderstorms and noise from distant thunderstorms. After listening to his recordings, however, he identified something he had never noticed before: a weak third sort of static that sounded more like a hiss.

Keen on tracing the origin of the hiss, Jansky constructed a better rotating antenna that looked similar to a merry-go-round—a circle of both vertical and horizontal metal rods with a rotation that allowed it to track the hiss. Jansky rotated his antenna and carefully measured the timing of the faint hiss. After looking at his findings, Jansky determined that the noise was not generated by an earthbound meteorological event.

Instead, he deduced that the faint hiss had to be coming from somewhere in the center of the Milky Way.

At the age of twenty-six, Jansky had made a historic discovery. As a physicist, Jansky understood that all forms of energy waves passing through the universe, including light, were electromagnetic waves of varying lengths. All are generated when atoms and molecules collide with each other, forming waves, much as a stone tossed into a pool of water forms waves. One of the characteristics of long radio waves that differentiate them from visible light waves is that they can be heard but not seen. Therefore, Jansky concluded that bodies deep in space could and did emit invisible light rays as well as visible ones.

Light waves that are characterized by a particular range of electromagnetic wavelengths between seven hundred and four hundred nanometers (a nanometers is one-billionth of a meter) happen to be visible to the human eye, yet they account for only a small fraction of the electromagnetic spectrum. All other light waves are either too long or too short to be seen. Those that are much longer, typically ranging from slightly less than one inch to hundreds of feet, fall into the spectrum called radio waves. Nonetheless, they are forms of electromagnetic light waves.

Jansky's fortuitous discovery gave birth to a new branch of astronomy called radio astronomy. He determined that all cosmic objects emit radio waves (as well as other energy waves) that can reveal just as much as, and often more than, visible light. Following Jansky's discovery, astronomers developed more sophisticated means of collecting radio waves than his rudimentary merry-go-round. These innovative devices allowed astronomers to gather radio waves, analyze them, and even convert them into spectacular photographs.

The First Radio Telescope

In 1937, Grote Reber, an American radio engineer, read about Jansky's work and set out to construct the first professional radio telescope. Reber understood that radio waves were no different from visible light waves except for their longer lengths and lower energy levels. With this information, he realized the best design for an efficient radio telescope would be to copy designs of existing optical telescopes.

Since radio waves can be very long, very large surfaces would be needed to capture and focus them. Mirrors made of lightweight and inexpensive wire mesh would be more practical than glass mirrors yet just as efficient for capturing the much longer radio wavelengths. Although the wire mesh mirrors have holes in them that visible light passes through, longer radio waves reflect off them just as visible light waves reflect off glass mirrors. Reber also understood that radio wave mirrors would require a focal point, but instead of it being an eyepiece, it would be a receiver capable of capturing and then amplifying the waves for recording and converting into photographs. The reason radio telescopes are so similar to visible light telescopes is because the physics of all electromagnetic energy is so similar; both visible light and radio waves move through space at the speed of light and both reflect off a variety of surfaces in the same way.

Reber's first radio telescope was a thirty-foot reflector mirror set up in his backyard in Illinois. Reber spent long hours every night scanning the skies with his telescope. He worked at night because in 1937 automobile engines emitted sparks out of their tailpipes that created too much interference during the daytime. At night, fewer people drove their cars and Reber could get better readings.

Success was a matter of trial and error. Reber designed the first telescope to detect wavelengths of about six inches, but it failed to detect any signals. The second one, designed for two-foot-long waves, also failed. Finally, he adjusted for six-foot waves and was successful in detecting signals from the Milky Way, confirming Jansky's earlier discovery. Reber continued his

investigations of radio sources and confirmed that they arose throughout the Milky Way. In 1944, he published the first maps of the galaxy based solely on radio waves.

Through his trials, Reber learned that his telescope was capable of detecting a broad spectrum of radio wavelengths and that he could tune it to locate and record specific ones of interest. He was also the first

In 1948 American radio engineer Grote Reber stands next to an enormous amplifier that captures and focuses radio waves emitted from celestial bodies in the Milky Way.

to recognize that much of deep space—which appears to be a blur of dust and gas storms when viewed with optical telescopes—can look extraordinarily detailed when viewed with radio telescopes. The reason for the greater resolution is that the longer wavelengths pass through the dust and gas of deep space, unlike visible wavelengths that are blocked or refracted.

How Radio Telescopes Work

Radio telescopes work with three basic components. Each must have a large metallic mirror (also called a dish or antenna), a focus point called the feed, and a sensitive radiometer or radio receiver. The sensitivity of a radio telescope—its ability to capture and analyze weak sources of radio waves—depends on the area and efficiency of the dish and the sensitivity of the receiver used to amplify the signals. Cosmic radio sources can be extremely weak because they sometimes emanate billions of light-years away. Since radio waves can be weak, observing times up to many hours are sometimes needed to capture their signals.

Weak radio waves also demand careful aiming of the mirror. In some radio telescopes the dish surface is equatorially mounted; one axis is parallel to the rotation axis of the earth. This mounting technique allows the telescope to follow a position in the sky as the earth rotates by moving the antenna parallel to the earth's axis of rotation.

Once properly aimed, the dish operates in the same manner as a television satellite antenna to capture and focus incoming radiation onto the feed that is suspended a few feet above the center of the dish. Radio waves are then transferred from the feed to the receiver by way of a coaxial cable. In the earliest form of radio telescope, such as that designed by Reber, the receiver was directly coupled to the feed, but today, the detected signal is carried away from the feed to a nearby electronics laboratory where it can be amplified, recorded, analyzed, and converted into pictures.

What Is Electromagnetic Radiation?

All forms of light are forms of electromagnetic radiation. Whether it is visible light the eye can detect, X-rays used by doctors to look at bones, radio waves that transmit music, or microwaves used to cook food, all are forms of electromagnetic radiation.

Radiation is produced throughout the universe when electrons, the tiny charged particles on the outer edges of atoms, make changes in their motion, usually by collisions with other rapidly moving atoms. These swift changes, similar to minuscule vibrations, produce bundles of energy called photons, which vary in energy levels and move across the universe at the speed of light.

Astrophysicists consider electromagnetic radiation to be both waves and photons, each distinct from the other. In all cases, the length of the wave is related to the energy contained in the photons; the shorter the wavelength, the higher the energy of the photons. The only difference between the various types of electromagnetic radiation is their wavelengths and the amount of energy found in their photons. Radio waves, for example, which can occasionally be miles in length, have photons with very low energies, while gamma rays, which rarely exceed one-millionth of an inch, have very high energies. As a point of comparison, the vibration energy required to produce a single gamma ray is billions of times more rapid than the vibration of a radio wave. Although this may sound like a massive amount of energy, the energy from hundreds of trillions of gamma rays would not be enough to light a single lightbulb, even for a second.

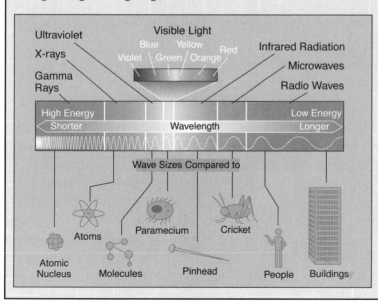

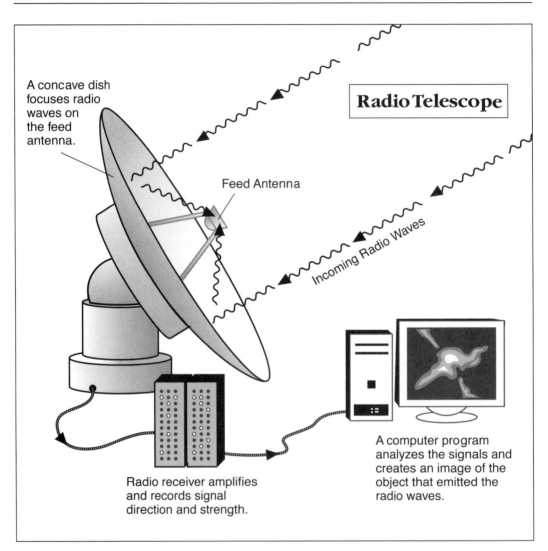

A concave dish focuses radio waves on the feed antenna.

Radio Telescope

Feed Antenna

Incoming Radio Waves

Radio receiver amplifies and records signal direction and strength.

A computer program analyzes the signals and creates an image of the object that emitted the radio waves.

The conversion of nonvisible waves into visible pictures is now performed by complex computer software programs. Their job is to take the amplified waves, determine their individual profiles based on several characteristics, assign a numeric value, and then convert their values into dots, called pixels, which are transferred onto photographic paper. Sometimes following hours of capturing distant radio waves, thousands of numeric values are combined by computers to form one dazzling color photograph of tens of thousands of pixels depicting an expansive galaxy swirling in a dense, gaseous region billions of light-years away.

The Big Ear

As the size of radio dishes grew to capture longer electromagnetic wavelengths from deeper space, a consortium of American radio astronomers stumbled across a naturally occurring concave depression in the earth's limestone surface in the mountainous jungle of Arecibo, Puerto Rico. In 1963, recognizing that this depression might be a perfect place to construct an enormous radio observatory, scientists began construction of a dish one thousand feet in diameter that was immediately dubbed "the Big Ear." Besides the natural depression, the surrounding jungle acted as a buffer to keep towns and highways at a safe distance, thereby minimizing terrestrial interference with incoming celestial signals. The giant size of the reflector is what makes the Arecibo Observatory unique. It is the largest telescope on the planet, which means it is also the world's most sensitive radio telescope. Other radio telescopes may require observing times of several hours to collect enough energy and data from a distant radio source, whereas at Arecibo such an observation may require just a few minutes.

Such a massive telescope embedded in the earth's crust has one major flaw: It cannot be aimed by rotating or tipping the dish. To resolve this problem, astrophysicists realized they would need to aim the telescope by moving the feed rather than the dish. The feed at Arecibo, which is suspended 450 feet above the dish, hangs in midair on eighteen cables. It is a bow-shaped structure 328 feet long that can be moved side to side and positioned anywhere up to twenty degrees from the vertical to focus on objects in deep space. Aiming the feed at a certain point above the dish enables radio emissions originating from a very small area of the sky in line with the feed to be accurately focused, thereby producing superb photographs.

The Arecibo Radio Telescope

Those who see the Arecibo radio telescope for the first time are astounded by the enormous size of the reflecting surface The huge spherical reflector is 1,000 feet in diameter and 167 feet deep, and covers an area of about twenty acres. The dish surface is made of almost forty thousand perforated aluminum panels, each measuring 3 feet by 6 feet, supported by a network of steel cables strung across the underlying dish to position them. Suspended 450 feet above the reflector is a nine-hundred-ton platform. Similar in design to a bridge, it hangs in midair on eighteen cables, which are strung from three reinforced concrete towers around the perimeter. Each tower is anchored to the ground with seven 3.25-inch-diameter steel bridge cables. Another system of three pairs of cables runs from each corner of the platform to large concrete blocks under the reflector. They are attached to giant jacks that allow adjustment of the height of each corner of the dish with millimeter precision.

Just below the triangular frame of the upper platform is a circular track on which the azimuth arm turns. Since the dish is embedded in the earth and cannot be rotated, the azimuth arm can be adjusted to point to particular positions in the sky. The azimuth arm is a bow-shaped structure 328 feet long that allows for positions anywhere up to twenty degrees from the vertical.

Hanging below the azimuth arm are various antennae, each tuned to a narrow band of frequencies. The antennae point downward and are designed specially for the Arecibo spherical reflector. Aiming a feed antenna at a certain point on the reflector allows radio emissions originating from a very small area of the sky in line with the feed antenna to be focused.

The massive radio telescope at Arecibo in Puerto Rico can detect the source of extremely distant radio waves.

The Arecibo telescope detects the source of radio waves more distant than any other radio telescope. It has scoured the cosmos from within the nearby solar system to within 5 percent of the edge of the universe, 12 billion light-years away. Arecibo studies the properties of planets, stars, comets, and asteroids within the Milky Way, as well as more exotic cosmic entities from the farthest reaches of the universe, such as supernovas and even black holes. Many of the radio waves emitted from deep space billions of light-years away arrive so weak that only the Big Ear can detect them. One of Arecibo's unique capabilities is its ability to analyze surface properties of distant objects by transmitting radar waves to them and then capturing the echo that bounces back. To perform such an operation, Arecibo possesses a one-megawatt planetary radar transmitter located in a special room. Following a short transmission period, the dish awaits the echo's return. Analyzing the returning echoes provides information about surface properties, the size of the targeted object, and its distance from Earth.

Yet, as the great astronomer and author Isaac Asimov noted about Arecibo and other large radio telescopes, "Even the largest radio telescopes are not very good at resolution if they are regarded as single structures in themselves. They can't be capturing the size of the wavelengths they deal with."[10] What Asimov meant by his comment was that radio wavelengths that exceeded the diameters of large telescopes were only partially captured, therefore part of the cosmic information is lost.

Fortunately for Asimov and all radio astronomers, Martin Ryle at Cambridge University in England had already begun work on a solution to that problem. In the late 1950s, he described a new science called interferometry that could link multiple telescopes, located many miles apart, to form a network of radio telescopes working as one to piece together any information from partially captured radio waves.

Long-Baseline Interferometry

Ryle understood that massive radio telescopes, many miles in diameter, were desirable but impossible to build. As an alternative, he proposed the ingenious solution that one could be synthesized by linking many smaller ones. Working in unison, their signals could be combined to produce cosmic maps and photographs far superior to those produced by Arecibo alone.

In 1964, Caltech initiated interferometry with twin dishes at the Owens Valley Radio Observatory in California. Each was ninety feet in diameter and mounted on railroad tracks so they could be moved varying distances from each other, with a maximum separation of sixteen hundred feet. Both were cabled together to a central data-gathering laboratory where the captured radio waves could be amplified and then combined to form a single stronger signal that could later be transformed into a photograph.

Astronomers were astonished when they realized that just thirty years following the initial discoveries of Jansky and Reber, radio telescopes had developed the best method for observing the universe in sharp detail. They mulled over their success and wondered what quality imagery they might achieve by using interferometry to link multiple telescopes together over greater distances. Such a notion, called long-baseline interferometry (LBI), was on the horizon.

By the mid-1970s, radio astronomers were eager to experiment with LBI to generate better resolution of distant objects. At the heart of LBI is a large array of multiple telescopes interconnected by interferometric equipment. Many new radio telescopes were constructed and are still in use. The largest is the Very Large Array (VLA) on the plains of San Agustin fifty miles west of Socorro, New Mexico.

The VLA

One of the world's premier astronomical radio observatories, the VLA consists of twenty-seven radio dishes

in a Y-shaped configuration. Each dish is eighty-two feet in diameter, weighs 230 tons, and is mounted on rails to provide movement. When data are electronically combined from the array, the resulting resolution is equivalent to a single antenna twenty-two miles in diameter.

The rails that provide movement for each antenna function the same as the zoom lens on a camera. By moving the antennae closer together or farther apart, astronomers can achieve either a wide-angle look into space or a tight telephoto view. Greatest detail is achieved when the array is at maximum disbursement. As the size of the array gradually decreases to the smallest spread, when the telescopes are all placed within four-tenths of a mile of the center, scientists achieve a wide-angle view of the overall structure of the object they are observing. By gathering wavelengths from the same distant object in multiple configurations, astronomers can capture a great deal more information.

The position of the twenty-seven radio telescopes of New Mexico's Very Large Array can be adjusted to measure wavelengths from distant objects in multiple configurations.

Today, configurations of the VLA are changed about every four months.

The development of long-baseline radio interferometry showed images of the sky that were significantly finer than anything previously. VLA reveals detail as if the observer were 100,000 times closer to the object. Barry Clark, who currently directs the scheduling for the VLA, commented:

> What [astronomers] want to do is to study everything from Jupiter to the most distant objects in the universe. Some of the most interesting results have come from regions where stars have recently formed, regions where stars have exploded, and regions of what might be supermassive black holes.[11]

During the early years of the twenty-first century, the long-baseline interferometer at the VLA has been used for a series of investigations into deep space, studying phenomena billions of light-years away. One recent project objective was to use the maximum capability of each of these telescopes to capture light from objects such as galaxies and quasars extremely far away and thus see them as they were when the universe was young. By comparing these ghost images from the early universe with the same type of objects at closer distances, and thus from a more recent past, astronomers can learn how these objects likely changed over billions of years.

A second function of the VLA is to make a detailed image of the supernova called 3C58. A supernova is the result of a cataclysmic explosion caused when a star exhausts its fuel and ends its life in a massive fiery fury. The new image of this debris from 3C58 will be compared with earlier images dating back to 1984 to learn how fast the material is moving outward from the explosion site and to monitor other changes in the supernova.

The success of the VLA using the latest interferometry tantalized the imaginations of astronomers. If telescopes spread over a twenty-two-mile baseline could improve the science of astronomy significantly, what might be the result of a baseline hundreds of times as long?

The Very Long Baseline Array

In the late 1980s, astronomers were ready to create a virtual radio telescope spanning thousands of miles. Using fundamentally the same interferometry and radio telescopes that were in use in Socorro, ten sites spanning the Pacific Ocean and the continental United States were selected as segments of the Very Long Baseline Array (VLBA).

Very Long Baseline Array

Brewster, Washington

Hancock, New Hampshire

Los Alamos, New Mexico

Owens Valley, California

North Liberty, Iowa

Kitt Peak, Arizona

St. Croix, Virgin Islands

Mauna Kea, Hawaii

Pie Town, New Mexico

Fort Davis, Texas

Ten radio telescopes function together as one instrument. Each is aimed and controlled remotely from an operations center in Socorro, New Mexico. The operations center also collects information from all stations to produce a single set of data.

In 1993, astronomers working for the National Radio Astronomy Observatory (NRAO) finished coordinating the network and began operating the VLBA, the world's largest telescope. Each of its ten sites is equipped with an eighty-foot dish antenna, and together they capture the same radio signals from deep space sources. The spread of the array, roughly five thousand miles, provides the VLBA with the highest resolution of any telescope. Astronomers working on the VLBA describe its resolution as being less than one milliarcsecond. This tiny angle corresponds to the width of a human hair as seen from ten miles. According to astronomers working on the VLBA, "This is equal to being able to read a newspaper in New York while standing in Los Angeles."[12]

The antennae, which operate unattended most of the time, are controlled by a single operator in Socorro. Astronomical data from the ten antennae are recorded on digital tape with the assistance of atomic clocks to capture precisely the same radio waves at each site. The atomic clocks are accurate to within one-billionth of a second per day, the equivalent of one second of deviation over 6 million years. The tapes are then shipped to Socorro where they are correlated by high-speed computers.

Since its inception, the VLBA has provided remarkably detailed photographs of the powerful cores of distant quasars, unusually bright remote objects that spew out tremendous amounts of energy. Before radio telescopes, quasars appeared to be simply bright distant stars, but with the VLBA, they are known to be millions of times brighter than stars. The VLBA has also provided precise measurements of the speed of debris from exploded supernovas at the cores of distant galaxies. Regarding the VLBA, astrophotographer Russ Dickman emphasizes,

Greater resolution is vital to astronomy because it shows more details, and details are clues to origins.

We have been looking at galaxy cores and quasars for a long time but we don't fully understand the processes. The key to what is happening is the core, near the central engine. That's because the "engine" —whether it's a black hole or some equally bizarre object—drives the entire galaxy.[13]

Physicists understood that if radio telescopes were effective at capturing long wavelengths, other types of telescopes might be capable of capturing very short wavelengths. Toward the end of the 1950s, while long-wave radio and midlength visible light telescopes were probing the depths of space making new discoveries, astrophysicists were wondering what else they might discover by studying very short wavelengths of light. Very short wavelengths, much shorter than visible light, were known to exist, but the problem facing the astronomy community was how to capture them. Their very short wavelengths, often one-hundredth the length of visible light, are rarely able to penetrate the earth's insulating atmosphere. For this reason, earthbound telescopes would be of little value.

By the beginning of the 1960s, however, when America began rocketing satellites far above the earth's atmosphere, astronomers saw them as a solution for capturing very short wavelengths.

Chapter 4

Observing the Violent Universe: X-rays and Gamma Rays

At the opposite end of the electromagnetic spectrum from low-energy, long radio waves are very high-energy, short X-rays followed by even shorter gamma rays, the shortest of all waves on the electromagnetic spectrum. As is the case with radio waves, X-rays and gamma rays are forms of light invisible to the eye. X-rays range in length from 1 to 100 nanometers, while gamma rays range from 0.1 to 0.001 nanometers. Wavelengths this short, some barely the diameter of individual atoms, explode across the universe with tremendous energy as a result of violent conflagrations in deep space. X-rays and gamma rays have several common characteristics besides their energy levels and lengths. An analysis of their origins reveals that they emanate from the hottest spots in the universe—regions where atoms have been raised to extremely high temperatures exceeding millions of degrees Fahrenheit. Temperatures this extreme are the result of violent collisions of atoms caused by cataclysmic explosions or heat-intense crushing gravitational fields capable of compressing stars one hundred

58

times the size of the sun into dense spheres a few miles in diameter.

Violent cosmic infernos can only partially be detected by the visible and radio waves they emit. To investigate their nature more fully, astronomers must study the most abundant electromagnetic energy they propagate, gamma rays and X-rays. By studying the spectra of these

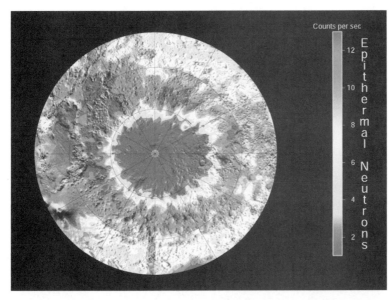

At top, Gamma-ray imaging produced this view of Mars; below, the Chandra telescope captured this image of the X-ray spectrum of a black hole.

waves, physicists can determine the composition of the objects that produced them, their age, and what part of the universe they came from. Professor Shri Kulkarni at Caltech suggests that there may be much more to be learned in the future when he says, "By relying on gamma rays or x-rays to tell us where and when an explosion is taking place, we may be exposing only the tip of the cosmic explosion iceberg."[14]

Astrophysicists have located sources of extreme heat and accompanying X-ray and gamma ray emissions in an astonishing variety of places ranging from the vast spaces between galaxies to some of the universe's most bizarre phenomena such as neutron stars (highly compressed collapsed stars), supernovas (exploding stars), and black holes (a collapsed star whose gravity is so strong that not even light can escape its pull). According to astronomers Wallace and Karen Tucker in their book *The Cosmic Inquirers: Modern Telescopes and their Makers*,

> The discovery of multimillion-degree gas around supernovas, neutron stars, black holes, and supergiant galaxies reinforced the view that violent events and high-energy processes play a crucial and quite possibly a decisive role in the structure and evolution of our universe.[15]

Although X-rays were discovered in 1895 and used by physicians to photograph bones and teeth, it was not until the late 1950s, when early satellites were catapulted into space, that astronomers began to design orbiting telescopes capable of capturing these waves and using them to provide a detailed analysis of the violent universe.

Designing Orbiting Telescopes

The most notable revolutionary characteristic of X-ray and gamma ray telescopes is the necessity of placing them in orbit high above the earth's insulating atmosphere. Even though the atmosphere consists of gases, dust, and moisture, its eighteen-mile depth is thick enough to absorb more than 99 percent of all X-rays and gamma rays. Astronomers explain that very short wavelengths passing through the atmosphere will encounter as many atoms as they would through a fifteen-foot-thick concrete wall.

One of the most formidable problems associated with satellite telescopes was providing sufficient electricity to operate a variety of motors, computers, and transmitters needed to run the instrument. Solving this problem required telescope satellites to orbit with a slight tilt toward the sun to absorb sunlight on solar panels made of thousands of thumb-sized photovoltaic cells. These cells, made of silicone, capture sunlight and then convert it to electricity used to power the telescope.

In addition to electrical needs, designers took into account temperature extremes that can daily plunge far below freezing when the satellite is shaded from the sun and then soar hundreds of degrees when it is exposed to it. Such wild fluctuations would damage fragile equipment were it not for thermostats and heating and cooling elements placed on the telescope and instruments. The thermostats measure external temperatures around the telescope and maintain internal temperatures between thirty-two and eighty-one degrees Fahrenheit.

Satellites were not the only unconventional component of very short wavelength astronomy. The physics of these short yet high-energy wavelengths meant that conventional reflecting mirrors, regardless of their composition, would not work. New unconventional light-capturing devices would be needed for both X-ray and gamma ray telescopes.

The Unconventional Design of X-ray Mirrors

X-rays do not reflect off mirrors in the same manner as visible or radio waves. Because of their high energy, X-rays that strike any surface directly will penetrate into it in much the same way that bullets striking

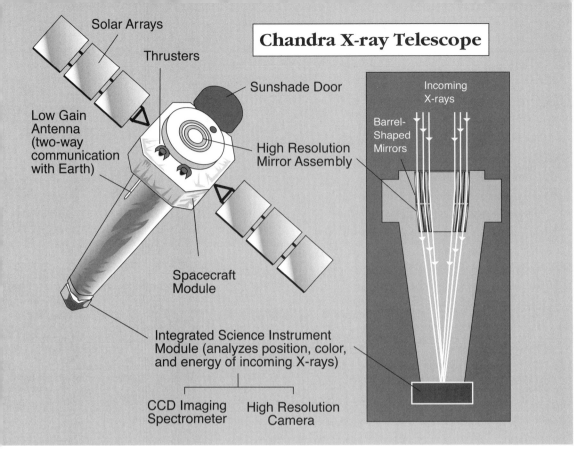

Chandra X-ray Telescope

Solar Arrays

Thrusters

Sunshade Door

Low Gain
Antenna
(two-way
communication
with Earth)

High Resolution
Mirror Assembly

Spacecraft
Module

Integrated Science Instrument
Module (analyzes position, color,
and energy of incoming X-rays)

CCD Imaging
Spectrometer

High Resolution
Camera

Incoming
X-rays

Barrel-
Shaped
Mirrors

wood embed into or penetrate its surface. Likewise, just as bullets can ricochet off a surface when they hit it at a grazing angle, so too will X-rays ricochet off mirrors if they hit at very shallow angles.

These properties forced optical engineers to construct X-ray telescopes that look more like barrels that slightly taper at one end. Typically, four mirror shells are nested inside one another almost parallel to the path of incoming X-rays so they ricochet rather than collide with mirrors. Once captured by detectors at the end of the nested mirrors, the X-ray data are then transmitted to Earth where they are analyzed and converted into mathematical values. These can then be used to produce photographs of the distant objects that produce the X-rays.

The barrel-shaped mirrors must be exceptionally smooth to ricochet exceedingly small X-rays. The surfaces of the mirrors vary by only ten-billionth of an inch so that no bumps interfere with the precise skip of the X-rays as they pass down the telescope and fall on the detectors. As a way of emphasizing the remarkable smoothness of the mirrors, astrophysicists at Caltech explain that if the earth's surface were as smooth as modern X-ray mirrors, the highest mountain on Earth (twenty-nine-thousand-foot Mt. Everest) would be less than six feet tall.

By the mid-1990s, X-ray astronomers readied the launch of their largest and most sensitive X-ray telescope, called Chandra, named in honor of Indian American Nobel laureate astrophysicist Dr. Subrahmanyan Chandrasekhar. On July 23, 1999, the National Aeronautics and Space Administration's (NASA) Chandra telescope was deployed by the space shuttle *Columbia*. Chandra flies two hundred times higher than most other orbiting telescope satellites, which places it in an elliptical orbit that averages about seventy- eight thousand miles from Earth, almost one-third the distance to the moon. Astronomers have used Chandra to collect X-rays in order to understand the birth and death of stars, the nature of black holes and neutron stars, and the formation and evolution of galaxies.

The Chandra Mission

The combination of Chandra's high-resolution, large collecting mirrors, and sensitivity to higher-energy X-rays is revealing secrets about extremely faint X-ray sources as they existed billions of years ago. Chandra has captured and analyzed X-rays from high-energy regions of the universe such as the remnants of exploded stars. It also has picked up a mysterious force opposing gravity that astronomers call "dark energy." Many astrophysicists believe that this oppositional energy is causing the current accelerated expansion of the universe.

Capturing X-rays from so many peculiar phenomena would be of no value to astronomers if they were unable to analyze and photograph them. Performing these two tasks occurs within the instrument. At the narrow far end of the satellite's cylinder ricocheting X-rays are captured for analysis on an imager consisting of two components: A high-resolution camera and a spectrometer that measures and analyzes energy levels. The high-resolution camera records X-ray images, giving scientists an unequaled look at violent, high-temperature events. The camera is composed of two clusters of 69 million tiny lead-oxide glass tubes. The tubes are only one-twentieth of an inch long and just one-eighth the thickness of a human hair. When an X-ray strikes a tube, it triggers an avalanche of about 30 million electrons. A grid of electrically charged wires at the end of the tube assembly detects this flood of electrons and precisely determines the position of its origin. By electronically determining the entry point of the original X-ray, the camera can produce an image of the object that produced the X-rays. As a result of this camera, Chandra has transmitted to Earth thousands of extraordinary photographs of brilliant cosmic explosions, thermal gas storms, matter being sucked

The Chandra X-ray Telescope orbits Earth in 1999. Chandra helps astronomers better understand the birth and death of stars and galaxies.

into black holes, and spinning high-energy phenomena. According to Harvey Tananbaum, director of the Chandra X-ray Observatory, "That's the excitement. Chandra shows us how spectacular the universe is."[16]

Near the camera is the spectrometer, which is capable of recording not only the position but also the color and energy of the X-rays from the observed object. These in turn are used to determine the target's distance from Earth. The spectrometer is made up of ten X-ray detectors similar to those used in home video recorders and digital cameras. The spectrometer can distinguish up to fifty different types of X-ray energies that contribute to determining the X-rays' spectrum, age, and distance to the source.

Determining the distance of stars and galaxies from Earth is crucial. This is accomplished by measuring what astrophysicists call an object's "cosmological redshift," that is, its shift in wavelength—an actual elongation of the wavelength as it travels through space— toward the red end of the spectrum. Scientists know that the more a wavelength is redshifted, the longer and farther it has been traveling through space.

During the last two decades of the twentieth century, astrophysicists began puzzling over the origin of powerful but seemingly different explosions than those generating normal levels of X-rays. From time to time, they noted a bizarre and unexplainable flash of light ripping across the cosmos. Analysis revealed the flashes to be bursts of gamma rays. Clearly, astronomers had stumbled on something new and unusual that would require a new and unusual type of telescope to view them properly.

Gamma Ray Telescopes

Gamma ray telescopes are unlike all others—most notably because they do not utilize mirrors to capture and focus incoming gamma waves. The reason mirrors cannot be used is because gamma rays strike objects with such force—10 million times more energy than visible light and a thousand times more energy than X-rays—that even the mirrors designed to deflect X-rays fail.

Gamma ray telescopes are of two fundamental types. The first are those called spectrometers. These are telescopes capable of capturing electromagnetic radiation in simple bucket-shaped instruments known to astronomers as "light buckets." These instruments collect many wavelengths of light and filter out the gamma rays. The gamma rays then pass through electrical detectors called scintillators, which are made of several layers of silicon semiconductors, similar to those used in computers. Scintillators convert the gamma rays into low-energy visible wavelengths that can be measured, analyzed, and photographed. The instant the conversion takes place, a visible and measurable spark is emitted. This is a physical property of the conversion process known to astronomers as scintillation. That spark is then captured and analyzed to determine its energy level and age. In this type of telescope, the scintillator does not directly analyze the gamma rays; it analyzes the scintillations.

The second class of gamma ray telescope is a detector that performs the task of gamma ray photography. Detectors of this type sense gamma rays passing through a scintillator and then are able to calculate the direction of the incoming photon and create a photographic image of it. One such telescope type, called the Compton Scatter Telescope, is a two-level instrument roughly the size of a fifty-five-gallon oil drum. In the top level, each incoming gamma ray collides with an electrical component similar to a scintillator that splits the photon, causing it to scatter much like an object scatters into pieces when struck by a bullet. The scattered photon fragments then travels down into a second level of material that completely absorbs them. Phototubes recording the two levels can then determine the amount of energy captured in each layer and calculate the energy of the

The Significance of the Redshift

Measuring the phenomenon of redshift is the only way astronomers can determine the size and age of the universe. Light traveling from far beyond the earth must cross space that astronomers know to be expanding. The expanding universe actually stretches light waves, just as if they had been drawn on the skin of an expanding balloon. As light waves travel and stretch, their colors shift toward the red end of the electromagnetic spectrum, giving them a reddish hue. If the universe were contracting, which it is not, light wavelengths would shrink toward the violet end of the spectrum, creating a "violetshift."

The redshift of astronomical objects is measured by comparing characteristic spectral lines of photons in them with spectral lines of similar photons measured in the laboratory. The principle established by the astronomer Edwin Hubble, known as Hubble's law, states that the higher the redshift, the more distant the object that emitted the light because it had traveled farther and therefore was stretched more by the expanding universe.

photon when emitted, the strength of any magnetic field, its age, and possibly the process that created it.

Tracking Down Gamma Ray Bursts

Every day, unusual but powerful explosions flash across the cosmos. Some last between a few milliseconds and a few tenths of a second; a few rare bursts may last for several seconds. These relatively rare phenomena, called gamma ray bursts (GRBs), shine hundreds of times brighter than the explosion of a typical supernova and as much as a million trillion times brighter than the sun. Such concentrations of gamma rays make GRBs the most intense energy sources in the universe. The energy release is so extreme that astrophysicists maintain that if the energy of a single millisecond burst could be harnessed and stored, the world's energy needs could be met for the next hundred billion years.

Just thirty years ago, when GRBs were first detected, they ranked among the greatest mysteries of the universe. Although small amounts of gamma rays had been detected coming from the sun, they did not deliver the punch of a GRB. At that time a burst was detected just once or twice a year, but today superior satellite telescopes detect roughly one per day from random directions in the sky. Based on recent studies, most GRBs appear to have originated some 10 billion years ago when the universe was very young.

One of the foremost gamma ray satellites presently orbiting the earth is the High-Energy Transient Explorer (HETE) telescope launched by NASA in 2000. Its principal mission is to detect GRBs, determine their location, and then relay that information within milliseconds of reception to other astronomers collecting visible, infrared, and radio wavelengths. These astronomers in turn, focus their various telescopes on the burst to capture, record, and photograph the many different wavelengths of electromagnetic radiation. Dr. George Ricker, principal scientist for the HETE mission, said of the telescope, "The unique power of HETE is that it not only detects a large sample of these bursts, but it also relays the accurate location of each burst in real time to ground-based optical and radio observatories."[17]

GRB 030329

On Saturday, March 29, 2003, at 6:37 A.M. eastern standard time, the HETE telescope awoke startled astronomers when its computers detected the most massive GRB ever reported. According to gamma ray astronomers, the only known cataclysmic event of greater magnitude was the big bang. For more than thirty seconds, the burst outshone all other sources of gamma rays, and its afterglow, secondary radiating visible light, was still over a trillion times brighter than the sun two hours later.

Named by astrophysicists GRB 030329, within less than a split second of detection, HETE nailed down a location and immediately relayed the coordinates to hundreds of astronomers around the world, allowing them to join the observation. Dr. Ricker commented, "This was our biggest one ever, and it didn't get away. With scores of observations now completed and more

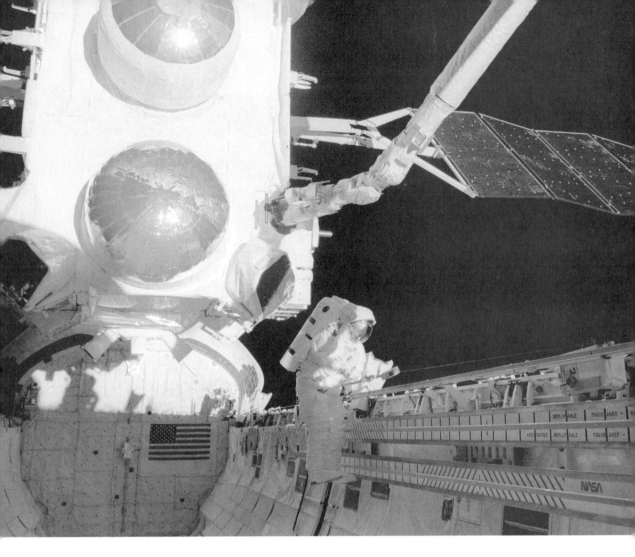

on the way, we should get a rather clear picture of what triggered this burst."[18] Observations poured in as scientists studied and then associated it with the emergent blast of a supernova. Astronomers were able to determine from the spectrum of this burst's optical afterglow that it occurred 2 billion years ago, relatively recently compared with the majority that date back as far as 10 billion years.

Astronomers cannot always determine what triggers a GRB, although the candidate list for such cataclysmic explosions is short. Some of the items on that list are what astronomers jokingly refer to as "weird stuff"— violent, imperfectly understood phenomena capable of generating extreme heat.

In 1991 an astronaut in the payload bay of the space shuttle Atlantis *prepares the* Compton Gamma Ray Observatory, *a powerful gamma ray telescope, for launch.*

Anatomy of Black Holes

Black holes, one of the strangest yet most intriguing astronomical phenomena, have all the characteristics of science fiction. Astronomers theorize with great certainty that black holes occur when the mass of a large star, several times the mass of the sun, runs out of fuel and collapses under its own weight until it compresses to a very small point. Under such conditions, gravity becomes so intense that not even light can escape.

A black hole does not have a surface in the same sense as the earth or sun does. A black hole does, however, have an invisible boundary called the event horizon, beyond which no telescope can see. This boundary is the point at which any matter, including light, will be sucked into the black hole, where it disappears from the sight of any outside observer. The diameter of the event horizon is very small, only about eighteen miles, compared with the diameter of the star before it collapsed, which would have been several million miles.

All matter sucked beyond the event horizon is doomed to be crushed as it descends ever deeper into the black hole's gravitational well, called the singularity. At this point, matter is compressed by the pull of gravity so intensely that all atoms are torn apart. In such an unimaginable environment, a single cubic inch of matter weighs several hundred billion tons. No visible light, X-rays, gamma rays, nor any other form of electromagnetism or particle, no matter how energetic, can escape the singularity. Black holes grow as they consume matter and their event horizons expand. A black hole in the center of a galaxy, where stars are densely packed, may attract other black holes and grow to the mass of a billion suns, at which point it becomes known as a super massive black hole.

Studying Weird Phenomena

When astronomers talk about "weird" phenomena, they are generally referring to a handful of cosmic events that have roughly three common characteristics: They involve stars, they radiate massive energy and gravitational waves across space, and they are only partially understood. The three most commonly studied weird phenomena are supernovas, neutron stars, and black holes. All three, it turns out, are related.

X-ray and gamma ray astrophysicists believe that each of these phenomena represents a stage in the deaths of stars. It is at these brief moments when stars burn out after billions of years that massive transformations of matter into energy occur. These transformations generate extreme heat, much like a massive thermonuclear bomb explosion. Although photographs can be taken of these death struggles utilizing all spectra of electromagnetic energy, astronomers are able to capture more useful data from X-rays and gamma rays than from the longer wavelengths.

As a star burns up its nuclear fuel, it loses its ability to support its own weight. At a critical point, the star begins to implode and die. If the star is particularly massive (larger than the sun, for example), the collapse accelerates and triggers a huge explosion known as a supernova. The explosion creates a blast wave that ejects the star's outer layers of dense gases into space,

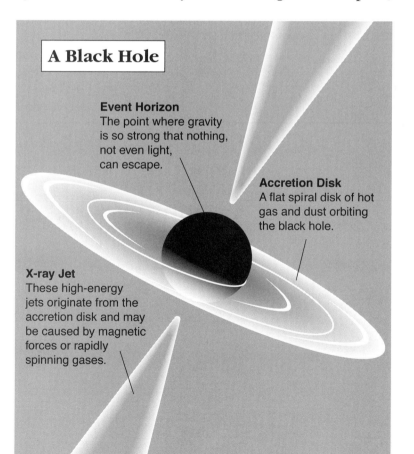

A Black Hole

Event Horizon
The point where gravity is so strong that nothing, not even light, can escape.

Accretion Disk
A flat spiral disk of hot gas and dust orbiting the black hole.

X-ray Jet
These high-energy jets originate from the accretion disk and may be caused by magnetic forces or rapidly spinning gases.

triggering a GRB. In November 2001, HETE detected one such GRB, and astrophysicist Shri Kulkarni at Caltech concluded, "With these observations we have tied this gamma-ray burst to an exploding star [supernova]. I am absolutely delighted that nature provided us with such a clean answer [cause]."[19] From the information gathered from the GRB, the scientists determined that the supernova occurred 5 billion light-years away.

Following the supernova stage, a dying star will collapse further. If the star was approximately twice the diameter of the sun, roughly 1.7 million miles, the remaining core collapses under intense pressure until nothing remains but neutrons densely packed into a diameter between ten and twenty miles wide. At this point the star becomes a neutron star so dense that as

An arrow marks the location of a white-colored gamma ray burst that may have occurred when a neutron star collapsed into a black hole.

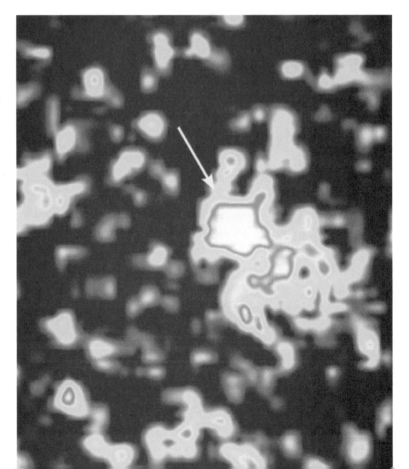

astronomer and author Frank Shu explains, "A sugar cube of neutron-star stuff on earth would weigh more than Mt. Everest!"[20] If, on the other hand, the dying star had a diameter ten times that of the sun or larger, following the supernova it will continue collapsing beyond a neutron star and become a black hole.

Black holes are phenomena whose cores become so dense, denser than a neutron star, that nothing, not even light, can escape their gravitational fields. For this reason, black holes cannot be seen because light that shines on them cannot bounce off. They can, however, be detected by the matter that their intense gravitational fields gobble up. As space matter swirls into a black hole, it generates intense heat that produces very short electromagnetic wavelengths. X-ray and gamma ray telescopes have detected several locations in the skies where massive dust and gas clouds have been photographed disappearing in a spiral swirl that seems to lead nowhere. According to Kelly Kizer Whitt, "The burst, named GRB 030329 resulted when a massive star ended its life and exploded, with its core collapsing inward to create a black hole."[21]

While X-ray and gamma ray physicists were exploring the cosmos with orbiting telescopes and making pioneering discoveries, physicists concentrating on lower-energy wavelengths saw similar opportunities to use space telescopes to gather visible light. Not since the construction of the Mt. Palomar Observatory had new optical telescopes been designed to explore and photograph deep space.

Chapter 5

Hubble

In 1962, the National Academy of Sciences recommended the construction of a large optical telescope. More revolutionary than any of its predecessors, however, this one would be the first telescope rocketed into orbit to capture visible light waves. Astronomers explained to all potential sponsors that a telescope would be placed in orbit a few hundred miles above the earth's polluted and distorting atmosphere, with a primary mirror one-half that of Palomar's yet capable of producing photographs ten times sharper. Delayed many years by congressional debate and then by the 1986 explosion of the *Challenger* shuttle, the Hubble Space Telescope (HST), named to honor the preeminent astronomer Edwin Hubble, blasted into orbit in 1990 and immediately became the world's most publicized and most talked about telescope.

Escaping Earth's enveloping atmosphere gives an orbital telescope three distinct advantages over land-based instruments. First, an orbital telescope does not lose light coming from outer space that is filtered out by the gases, moisture, and dust swirling in the earth's atmosphere. Second, it is not affected by distortions created by rising heat from the earth's surface. And third, it only collects light produced by celestial objects, not from the electric light of metropolitan centers that mix with and degrade light from space. According to astronomers Daniel Fisher and Hilmar Duerbeck in their book *Hubble: A New Window to the Universe*, "Large telescopes on earth can get nowhere close to [Hubble's] resolution. Only a telescope in space can deliver stellar images of a few hundredths of an arcsecond."[22]

American astronomers outlined five principal objectives for the HST: "Explore the Solar System, measure the age and size of the universe, search for our cosmic roots, chart the evolution of the universe, and unlock the mysteries of galaxies, stars, planets, and life itself."[23] Accomplishing such diverse objectives required a telescope that was capable of making, on the one hand, minute geological observations of small asteroids and comets little more than a few hundred feet across, while on the other hand studying and photographing super galaxy clusters billions of times larger than asteroids and comets in hopes of revealing the origins and destiny of the universe.

Construction

The HST is a telescope, but more than that, it is a satellite. A cylinder forty-three feet long, fourteen feet in diameter, and weighing 24,500 pounds, the HST is roughly the size of a school bus. Operating in the vacuum of space far from helping human hands, the satellite was constructed to accommodate some of the most technically complex astronomical instrumentation ever built.

To operate in space, the HST needs a power supply, communications equipment, computers, and a control system. Power is supplied by two 25-foot-long solar panels (384 square feet), each containing 48,760 individual photo cells. Together, the two panels are capable of generating 2,800 watts, roughly the equivalent of twenty-eight standard lightbulbs. The power generated by the panels is also used to charge six nickel-hydrogen batteries that provide power to the spacecraft for about twenty-five minutes per orbit while Hubble flies through the earth's shadow.

Designers of the Hubble Space Telescope had to take into account the conditions in which it was to operate. Hubble would be subject to the rigors of zero gravity and

Edwin Hubble

One of the great pioneers of modern astronomy, the American astronomer Edwin Powell Hubble was born in 1889 in Missouri. He began his adult life by earning a law degree and serving in World War I. However, after practicing law for one year, he decided to turn to astronomy. He completed a PhD dissertation, "The Photographic Investigation of Faint Nebulae," at the University of Chicago and then continued his work at Mt. Wilson Observatory in Pasadena, California, studying the faint patches of luminous "fog," or nebulae, in the night sky.

Using the largest telescope of its day, an eight-foot reflector, he studied Andromeda and a number of other nebulae and proved that they were other galaxies similar to our own Milky Way. He devised the classification scheme for galaxies that is still in use today, and he obtained extensive evidence that the laws of physics outside the galaxy are the same as on Earth—verifying the principle of the uniformity of nature. In 1929, using a one-hundred-inch telescope, he analyzed the speeds of recession of a number of galaxies and showed that the speed at which a galaxy moves away from the Milky Way is proportional to its distance. The explanation for this was apparent, yet revolutionary; he had proved that the universe is expanding, a principle now called Hubble's law.

Using this one-hundred-inch telescope, Edwin Hubble collected data that proved the universe is expanding.

temperature extremes that fluctuated several hundred degrees Fahrenheit during each trip around the earth. To protect its delicate instruments, Hubble is cloaked in a cocoon of multilayered insulation that shields the interior from extreme temperature fluctuations.

Hubble's optical system is held together by a truss system 17.5 feet in length and 9.5 feet in diameter. The whole optical unit weighs just 252 pounds because it is made of the space-age material graphite epoxy, the same material used in many of the latest golf clubs, tennis rackets, and bicycles. Graphite epoxy is a stiff, strong, and lightweight material that resists expanding and contracting in temperature extremes.

The most sensitive object in need of thermal protection is the mirror. Highly sensitive to temperature change, it must remain within a narrow temperature range to produce images that will answer astronomers' most profound questions about the universe.

The Hubble Mirror

The heart of the HST is its 94-inch-diameter Cassegrain mirror with a 24-inch center hole. Construction and assembly of the space mirror was a painstaking process spanning almost a decade. Corning Glass Works fabricated the 13-inch-thick blank mirror made of ultra-low expansion glass. To accommodate changing temperatures, they designed it in the form of a sandwich that had a honeycomb core (alternating hexagonal sections of glass and hollow voids) 10 inches thick fused between 1.5-inch-thick solid glass front and back plates. In addition to allowing the glass to expand and contract without cracking, this design reduced the weight. A solid core mirror blank of the same size would weigh 12,000 pounds; Hubble's weighed only 2,400 pounds. The cooling processes took three months to drop from the 2,156 degrees Fahrenheit liquid mass down to room temperature.

The cooled blank was then shipped to the optical facilities of Perkins-Elmer, the company contracted to

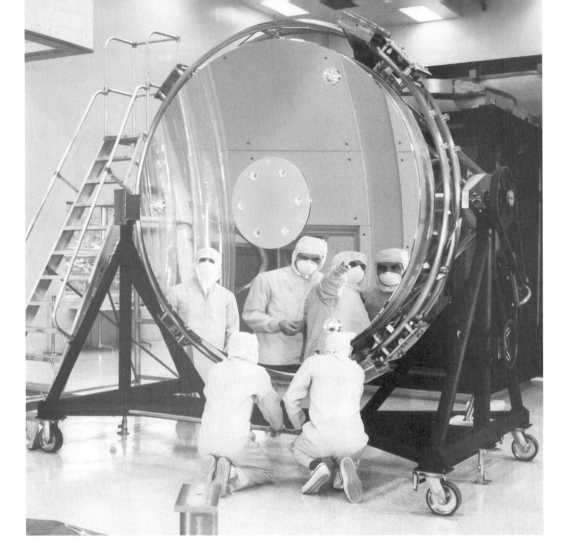

Researchers inspect the Hubble Space Telescope mirror. Construction of this massive mirror was a complex procedure that took nearly ten years to complete.

shape the mirror blank on a large grinder equipped with special diamond-tipped cutting tools and sophisticated polishers. Engineers trimmed the front and back plates, rounded the inner and outer diameter edges, and in the process reduced the front and back plate thickness from 1.5 inches to 1 inch. This reduced the mirror's weight to 1,700 pounds. Finally, highly skilled opticians using manually controlled tools and delicate hand-polishing techniques removed an additional 0.03 of an inch from the mirror's surface. The average time for each polish and test cycle was six days. During the many grinding and polishing cycles, the mirror was supported on an inflatable air bag device. Engineers deflated the air bag for polishing and inflated it for testing to simulate the gravity-free condition of an orbiting space telescope.

Laser tools were then used to polish the surfaces so that they would not deviate from the desired curve by more than 1/800,000th of an inch. To emphasize this precision, if Hubble's mirror were scaled up to the diameter of the earth, any leftover bumps on the glass would be no more than 6 inches high.

In order to make certain that the mirror was precisely ground, the optical engineers built a testing device known as a reflective null corrector. This device consisted of two small mirrors with a lens hung above the Hubble mirror. A laser beam was then shown on the main mirror through the lens of the corrector, which created a particular light pattern. When the mirror was ground to exactly the right shape, the light pattern would indicate to the optical engineers that they had achieved the desired curvature.

Blurred Vision

When the HST was launched, an optimistic NASA spokesperson called the telescope a new window on the universe. Entering orbit, all systems functioned properly when astronomers sent the remote signal to open the door that covered the telescope optics to take the first picture. The so-called first light occurred on May 20, 1990.

The photographs transmitted back to Earth successfully, yet experienced astronomers found the images disturbing. They were the wrong shape. Engineers attempted to adjust the lens, but after several weeks they recognized that something was seriously wrong. As more blurred photos poured in, astronomer Eric Chaisson inspected the faulty images and later recalled, "I sensed a total deflation in my gut."[24]

Hubble's main mirror was the wrong shape and could not focus properly. Engineers inspected an identical backup mirror and discovered than the central region of the mirror was too flat by just a few nanometers. This mistake severely reduced the resolution of the telescope so that when focused, it was able to gather only about 15 percent of the light of a very distant star instead of the 80 percent needed to produce a clear image.

The mistake was devastating to the $1.5 billion project. The mirror itself could not be repaired or exchanged deep in space, so NASA engineers went to work to develop corrective optics for Hubble's mirror.

Hubble's Contact Lens

No solution was possible without sending astronauts to make the repairs during a space walk. Optical engineers fabricated the Corrective Optics Space Telescope Axial Replacement (COSTAR) to correct the defective mirror. COSTAR was essentially a contact lens for Hubble's huge eye.

In December 1993, astronauts flew to the HST on the space shuttle *Endeavour*, carrying COSTAR and the necessary tools to install it. COSTAR consisted of five small mirrors that intercepted the beam from the flawed mirror, corrected the defect, and then relayed the corrected beam to the scientific instruments at the focus of the mirror. The procedure, although risky for the astronauts performing the installation, was completed without a hitch.

On December 18, 1993, just after midnight, astronomers packed a small room and huddled around a computer screen anxiously awaiting the first-light picture taken with HST's corrective lens. At 1:00 A.M., the tension broke when the image of a star popped onto the computer screen; the pinpoint dot of light meant that the star was clearly resolved. The telescope was fixed, and in the words of Ed Weiler, NASA's chief Hubble astronomer, it was "fixed beyond our wildest expectations."[25]

The in-orbit repair of Hubble was one of the landmarks of manned spaceflight. Installation of the COSTAR mirrors required an unprecedented series of five space walks on a single space shuttle flight. The

result of adding the corrective lens, however, was worth it. In his book *Hubble's Universe: Portrait of Our Universe*, Simon Goodwin noted that the COSTAR corrections "would enable the HST to resolve the disc of a five-cent piece from a distance of over 2 km [1.24 miles], and to create a sharpness of vision equal to a person's ability to stand in New York City and distinguish two fireflies, three feet apart in San Francisco."[26]

First the problem, then its resolution, and finally spectacular photographs made Hubble the most talked about telescope ever constructed. Mario Livio, a senior scientist with the HST, commented, "Ask any person the name of a playwright. Most of them would say Shakespeare. Ask them the name of a scientist.

An astronaut on the space shuttle Endeavour *uses a device to position his partner above the HST, where he installed the COSTAR lens to correct the telescope's defective mirror.*

Most of them would say Einstein. Ask the name of a telescope. They will all say Hubble."[27] Once Hubble was ready to go, astronauts turned their cameras into deep space to capture dramas never before seen.

Hubble's Cameras

HST carries an array of four different types of cameras, all of which are mounted on an apparatus capable of positioning them, one at a time, at the end of the mirror to produce photographs. Three are responsible for capturing visible light and one for infrared, the slightly longer wavelength just beyond visible light. Each of the four cameras has a different function.

The Near Infrared Camera and Multi-Object Spectrometer (NICMOS) is used to reveal information about the birth of stars, distant solar systems, and galaxies only available in infrared. Because NICMOS's advanced detectors must be kept cool to work best, they are contained in a large thermos bottle, called a dewer, which is chilled with liquid nitrogen to –351 degrees Fahrenheit.

The Space Telescope Imaging Spectrograph (STIS) camera records all lengths of the visible light spectrum. A prism called a spectrograph divides light into its component colors. This provides a "fingerprint" of a celestial object and gives information about its temperature, chemical composition, and motion, among many other characteristics. STIS is unique because it can sample some five hundred points along a large astronomical object simultaneously. This means that many regions in a planet's atmosphere or many stars within a galaxy can be recorded in a single exposure. STIS observations will lead to a greater understanding of the origin and evolution of galaxies and star formation. The most unusual camera, and the one of interest to black hole hunters, is the Advanced Camera for Surveys (ACS). The ACS maps the distribution of black holes throughout the Milky Way by detecting distant objects and gases swirling into their intense gravitational fields.

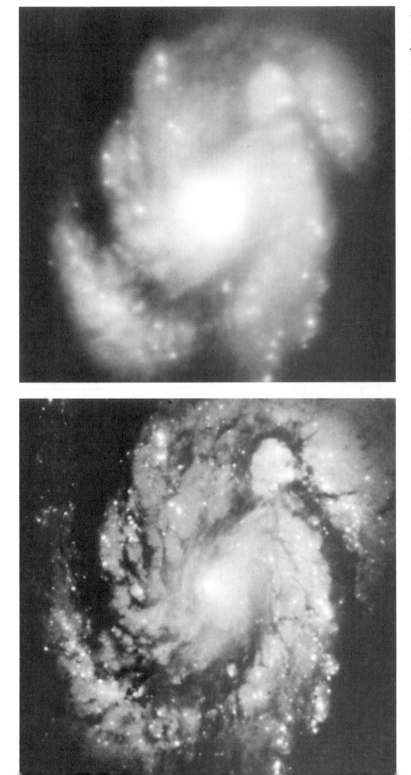

Above, this blurry image of a spiral galaxy was taken by the HST before COSTAR was installed; below, the same galaxy is imaged by the HST after the corrective lens was mounted.

Pinpoint Telescope Aiming

Photographing celestial objects in deep space requires pinpoint aiming, which necessitates an exceptionally stable telescope. Astronomers compare photographing distant stars and galaxies from a satellite to photographing bathers at a beach from a distant bobbing boat. Besides the uncertainty of movement, exposure times needed to capture faint light from deep space can last up to many hours. During that lengthy exposure, the telescope must maintain the same precise view angle toward the object or the photograph will be blurred. Just as telescopes anchored to the earth, Hubble must produce the same unwavering stability while floating in a weightless environment.

Accomplishing absolute stability for a long-duration photograph of several hours requires the work of six onboard gyroscopes. Each maintains the satellite's stability by spinning nineteen thousand times per minute, and each contains electronic sensors to detect any minute deflections of the gyroscope. If any deflection is detected, the sensors reposition the satellite.

Hubble's Accomplishments

Hubble's discoveries have revolutionized astronomy and astrophysics by providing the best understanding yet of the origins and the probable fate of the universe. The HST has afforded many of the most astonishing photographs ever taken of the cosmos. The images are like nothing ever seen before, depicting a universe more explosive and fantastic than anyone had imagined. In late 2003, for example, a single photograph taken by Hubble revealed the largest extent of the universe ever photographed, ten thousand galaxies covering 13 billion light-years. Since the light was just reaching Hubble, the picture showed the universe the way it looked near the dawn of time.

Other photographs reveal everything from razor-sharp views of the planets in the solar system to vast stellar regions where stars and planets are born. Some show the explosive outbursts of supernovas, while others show the swirling masses of stars that make up galaxies billions of light-years away from Earth. In 2004, astronomers were treated to photographs of reddish rectangular ladderlike structures surrounding a dying star. Dubbed the "Red Rectangle," its color and form are unlike that of any other known cosmic object. According to astronomers, its ladderlike appearance is the result of outflows ejected from the star in two opposing directions. In the same year, Hubble photographed sheets of debris from a stellar explosion in a neighboring galaxy that resembled the puffs of smoke and sparks from a summer fireworks display. Astronomers explain that the solar system was constructed from similar exploding debris in the Milky Way billions of years ago.

In 2003, Hubble taught astronomers about the creation of galaxies. Photographs detected a grouping of galaxies engaging in an act of consolidation. The galaxies are so tightly packed together that gravitational forces are beginning to rip stars from one and send them into another. Those gravitational forces, say astronomers, will eventually pull the galaxies together to form one super galaxy. Yet other recent data provided by the HST have provided insights into star formation. Photographs and spectral analyses suggest that the first stars in the universe appeared in an abrupt eruption of star formations, rather than at a gradual pace.

The thousands of photographs and millions of bits of data beamed down from the HST have also answered some fundamental questions about the universe. According to Dr. Bruce Margon, the associate director of science for the Hubble Space Telescope, Hubble has taught science a great deal: "Well, for one thing, how old is the place we live in? That used to be the subject of furious arguments amongst astronomers. It's almost an obsolete question now. Hubble has solved that."[28] By focusing the HST for 192 hours on the single most

The Deepest Photo of Space

On March 9, 2004, astronomers working with the Hubble telescope unveiled the most distant portrait of the visible universe ever achieved. Named the Hubble Ultra Deep Field (HUDF), this photograph revealed images of the first galaxies to emerge shortly after the big bang, a time when the first stars reheated the cold, dark universe. This historic new view is actually two separate images, one taken by Hubble's Advanced Camera for Surveys (ACS) and the other by its Near Infrared Camera and Multi-Object Spectrometer (NICMOS). Both images, when combined, reveal galaxies that are too faint to be seen by ground-based telescopes. In an interview found on the Web site HubbleSite.org, project manager Massimo Stiavelli states, "Hubble takes us to within a stone's throw of the Big Bang itself." Referring to the image studded with a wide range of galaxies of various sizes, shapes, and colors, Stiavelli adds, "There is a zoo of oddball galaxies littering the field. Some look like toothpicks; others like links on a bracelet."

The HUDF required a series of exposures taken over the course of four hundred Hubble orbits around the earth. Photons of light from the very faintest objects arrived at a trickle of one photon per minute, compared with millions of photons per minute from nearer galaxies. The photograph will be used to search for galaxies that existed between 400 million and 800 million years after the big bang—a relatively short period of time when compared with the 14-billion-year age of the universe.

distant white dwarf star, a star that died out billions of years ago, astronomers have determined the age of the universe to be about 13.8 billion years.

The picture of the universe became even more interesting and complicated when Hubble detected that the rate at which the universe is expanding has accelerated over time. When asked about the implications of this startling finding, Dr. Ed Weiler remarked, "It means that we don't understand gravity. This implies there's some negative energy force, some antigravity that's actually pushing things apart. We don't understand it. It's not supposed to be there."[29] The implications of this discovery are startling for cosmologists because it means that the universe may have no boundaries and that it therefore may expand forever.

Chapter 6

Peering into the Future

The astonishing success of the Hubble, Chandra, and HETE telescopes whetted astronomers' appetites for resolving more complicated mysteries about the universe. Unraveling these mysteries will require further discoveries about the universe, which, in turn, will require more efficient, improved, and exotic telescope designs.

Just as Galileo turned Old Discoverer to the Milky Way to discover that the blur of lights was actually millions of individual stars, twenty-first-century astronomers must continue to experiment to improve upon optics and telescope designs if further discoveries are expected. Fortunately for the future of science, newer, more unusual, and improved telescopes capable of discoveries that eclipse those of a decade or two ago are already either in orbit or scattered about the earth's surface. Indeed, telescopes are no longer just for discovering more galaxies, black holes, and supernovas; they are also being designed to conduct exotic experiments, to search for alien intelligent life, and possibly to locate a planet for future colonization.

Telescopes as Time Machines

From a remote outpost on the summit of Hawaii's dormant Mauna Kea volcano, astronomers at the W.M. Keck Observatory probe the deepest regions of the universe

Located at the top of Hawaii's Mauna Kea volcano, the twin Keck telescopes allow astronomers to study objects nearly 13 billion light-years away.

with unprecedented power and precision. Jointly built by scientists at the University of California, Caltech, and NASA at the end of the 1990s, their instruments are the twin 10-meter (394- inch) Keck telescopes—one, the world's largest optical telescope lens and the other, the world's largest infrared lens.

Working in unison, each lens operates with nanometer precision to look at faint objects an estimated 13 billion light-years away. Such faint galaxies are being viewed at a time only 800 million years after the big bang, when the universe was barely 6 percent of its current age. Dr. Frederic Chaffee, director of the Keck Observatory, makes the analogy that "telescopes are virtual time machines, allowing our astronomers to look back to the early history of the cosmos, and these marvelous observations are of the earliest time yet."[30]

At the heart of each Keck telescope is a revolutionary primary mirror, each of which captures different wavelengths of light, and combines them, using computers, into one image. Describing this unique design Keck astronomers say, "The two telescopes give astronomers the ability to resolve cosmic objects as though they were using a single mirror 85 meters [3,349 inches] in diameter."[31] The mirrors are synchronized to an accuracy of 30 nanometers, and that precision allows scientists to view the faintest stars in the most distant galaxies. Many of these observations are part of NASA's Origins program dedicated to the search for the earliest evidence relating to the birth of the universe. According to astronomer Sandra Faber, "Great telescopes like the Kecks allow us to explore the River of Time back toward its source. The Kecks will allow us, like no other telescope in history, to view the evolving universe that gave us birth."[32]

The secret to the Kecks' ability to see deep into space is the wizardry of their mirror design. The twin mirrors are enormous, yet neither is a single mirror. Each is composed of thirty-six individual hexagonal segments that move in concert as a single piece of reflective glass. Each

An astronomer cleans dust from one of Keck's hexagonal mirrors. Each of the two telescopes uses thirty-six of these mirror pieces.

segment is stabilized by a system of support structures and adjustable warping harnesses. During observations, a computer-controlled system of sensors and actuators (precision pistons) adjusts the position of each segment relative to its neighbors to an accuracy of four nanometers. This twice-per-second adjustment effectively counters any slight distortion from temperature variation or vibration from the earth's rotation.

Chilling the interiors of the insulated observatory domes during the day controls temperature variations that could induce deformation of the telescope's steel and mirrors. This is a big task; each dome contains more than 700,000 cubic feet of volume. Giant air conditioners run constantly during the day, keeping dome temperatures at or below freezing. At night when the dome is opened, exposing the telescope to the frigid night air, the telescope already is at the ambient outdoor temperature.

Are We Alone?

The revolutionary design of adjustable mirror segments was not the only radical mirror design for twenty-first-century astronomers. On a mountaintop in Arizona, the world's largest pair of binoculars scans the night sky. What these gargantuan binoculars are looking for might be more astonishing than what they look like.

In the mid-1990s, it seemed nothing new could be imagined for telescopes. There were already a proliferation of them in space and on land, and multiple telescopes connected by interferometric electronics seemed the height of innovation. Yet, optical engineers suggested still another new idea that neither Galileo nor Edwin Hubble could have imagined. They suggested, and later built, a binocular telescope on Mt. Graham, Arizona, called the Large Binocular Telescope (LBT).

The LBT looks much like massive binoculars. It consists of two 8.4-meter (331-inch) primary mirrors that are mounted in a single structure separated by just 47 feet. The mirrors can be used independently or as

The Search for a New Home

Lately, many people have begun wrestling with the question of whether humans should begin a search for a new home far from the earth's polluted environment. Alan Dressler is one of several astronomers who have discussed such a search, and the following statement can be found on the Web site Origins (www.origins.jpl.nasa.gov):

It will require ambitious telescopes to detail the conditions of such a world with evidence for seas and continents, and seasonal variations. We cannot yet know whether the worlds we seek are common or exceedingly rare, so our journey may eventually involve great flotillas of large telescopes that can extend the search to thousands or tens of thousands of stars. If the will and spirit hold, physics says it can be done.

Will we humans leave our home in the Solar System and begin to migrate over the Milky Way as we once spread over the earth? From our view at the beginning of this new century it seems both inevitable and impossible. But, if we find, in the orbit of a neighboring star, a planet resembling earth, one where human beings might conceivably live, the quest could become an obsession. Perhaps our descendants will praise us for our initiative, perhaps they will curse the relentless curiosity that propels humans into greater accomplishments and greater peril. We go on.

binoculars by sending the light of both mirrors to a single camera between the telescopes. At a remote 10,700-foot elevation, atmospheric conditions are excellent for capturing visual light. Used in its dual capacity, the LBT will be able to create extraordinarily sharp pictures of distant planets ten times smaller than those photographed by the HST.

The astronomers have many goals for this telescope, one of which is very different from all others and sounds more like science fiction than science. It is to locate planets that revolve around a star, just as Earth revolves around the sun. Such findings, astronomers believe, may reveal planetary systems suitable for supporting life. In fact, locating such a planet may suggest that other beings could exist in the universe. It may also contribute to the future colonization of other planets as humans migrate into space.

Perhaps the biggest problem faced by LBT astronomers intent on detecting planets orbiting a star is that the parent star is significantly brighter than the planet and, as seen by telescopes, the planet is extremely faint by comparison. This problem makes it imperative to eliminate the glare from the star to study any orbiting planets. The revolutionary technique developed to accomplish this, called nulling interferometry, allows the LBT to filter out the starlight to provide high resolution images of the planets.

Determining whether humans are alone in the universe might be determined by the LBT as it scans the sky for habitable planets, or it might be determined by waiting for aliens on a foreign planet to locate us. Some astronomers, who believe alien life might be more technilogically advanced than our own, have built telescopes in anticipation of their contacting us.

The Search for Extraterrestrial Intelligence

In 1984, a group of astronomers associated with the University of California's Berkeley campus began using telescope technology in an unorthodox way. They founded an astronomy institute called the Search for Extraterrestrial Intelligence (SETI), whose purpose is to search for and hopefully detect electromagnetic signals beamed throughout the universe from intelligent beings beyond the solar system.

SETI scientists believe that life on Earth suggests that given a suitable environment and sufficient time, life could have developed on other planets. They further expect that since there are an estimated 100 billion stars in the Milky Way galaxy, and that billions of galaxies exist in the universe, there ought to be many planets like Earth where intelligent aliens thrive. Whether intelligent technological civilizations exist is only speculation, yet if they exist, their attempts to contact others may be humankind's only hope for discovering them. To detect possible communications from space, SETI has deployed several telescopes, each detecting and recording different electromagnetic wavelengths.

What kind of signals are these scientists likely to receive? According to SETI astronomer Ron Hipschman, "There are really two possibilities. Either the other civilizations are intentionally sending out a signal that is expressly meant to get our attention, or, like us, they just happen to be doing their own business and some of their signals are 'leaking out.'"[33] As an example, Hipschman points out that over the past fifty years or so, all broadcast television shows have been radiating out from Earth at the speed of light; the earliest broadcasts have already traveled fifty light-years, roughly 300 trillion miles, from Earth. Although not yet very far compared to the billions of light-years between galaxies, at some point in time they may be detected by intelligent beings who may wish to signal back. What will an alien signal be like? Hipschman admits no one knows:

> We can scarcely imagine their thought processes, or their reasons and methods for communicating with us. All we can do is make some educated guesses based on our own knowledge and technology. And even if we are wrong about the aliens' reasoning, we can still hope that they will try to tailor their signal to our own naïve expectations.[34]

One assumption made by SETI astronomers is that any signal from space will be initially weak, gain in strength, and then fade away, all in the span of twelve seconds. This is because it takes twelve seconds for the Arecibo radio telescope's beam to scan any given point in the sky. During that time span an alien signal will initially be at the edge of the reception beam and therefore will be weak. It will become stronger and ultimately peak when the beam is aimed directly at the signal's source and finally it will fade away as Arecibo moves on to search other points in the sky.

Has SETI received anything approximating a signal from space? Yes, say directors, but just once. On August

Jill Tater, SETI's director, poses with a model for a new radio telescope array that may help in the search for extraterrestrial life.

15, 1987, a volunteer studying computer printouts of radio waves noted a signal so strong that it overwhelmed the normal transmissions. Astronomers who studied the signal believe it was a rather uninteresting series of numbers and letters translated as 6EQUJ5. Although SETI astronomers believe that it could have come from deep space, they also understand it might have been part of a secret encrypted American military message that they accidentally captured. Thus, the search continues.

GALEX: Mapping the Universe

On April 28, 2003, a new satellite telescope named the Galaxy Evolution Explorer (GALEX) was launched into space 428 miles above the earth's surface to answer two new fundamental questions about the universe: How do stars form, and are today's galaxies different from galaxies during the early universe? Anne Kinney, director of astronomy and physics in NASA's Office of Space Science, commented, "The Galaxy Evolution

Explorer is crucial to understanding how galaxies, the basic structures of our universe, form and function."[35]

Now halfway through its twenty-nine-month mission, GALEX has studied the nature and history of stars and galaxies and has begun to provide the first all-encompassing map of the universe. Dr. Christopher Martin, the project's principal investigator and an astrophysicist at Caltech, added, "This mission will provide the first comprehensive map of a universe of galaxies under construction and bring us closer to understanding how they and our own Milky Way were built."[36] Equipped with a technologically advanced ultraviolet telescope, to detect wavelengths slightly shorter than visible light, the spacecraft has been able to concentrate on young galaxies that actively create stars. After just one year of study, GALEX has witnessed the birth of stars. What appears to occur is that thin clouds of hydrogen, helium, and dustlike interstellar particles act as the raw materials of future stars. As clouds of interstellar particles attract other particles, they gradually increase in size. Eventually, gravity causes the cloud to collapse, causing intense heat. When the temperature reaches about 10 million degrees, a nuclear reaction begins and the star is born. This period of evolution, known as the contraction phase, can take as much as 500 million years for a star the size of the sun.

Scientists hope GALEX will provide an understanding how the chemical elements that make up the Milky Way were formed. Thus far, after only one year of studying galaxies, GALEX has confirmed one existing theory about star formation and contributed new findings that will increase current understandings about the birth of stars. Dr. Martin revealed two of GALEX's most important discoveries:

First, we have found evidence to support an existing theory that older galaxies—those formed during the first half of the life of the universe—produced stars more prodigiously than galaxies

GALEX, a satellite telescope, provided this image of two distant galaxies in 2003. GALEX is providing astronomers with a comprehensive map of the universe.

formed during the second half. Second, and unexpectedly, GALEX has located a relatively small number of fairly new galaxies, just a few hundred million years old, that for some inexplicable reason are forming stars at a much higher rate than other galaxies the same age. At this time, we do not know why.[37]

By the time the GALEX mission ends, Dr. Martin and his staff hope to understand why star formation peaked 7 billion years ago yet explain why a very few newer galaxies continue to produce stars at unusually high rates.

Testing Albert Einstein's Theory

Not all telescopes, regardless of their unique designs, are seeking to answer direct questions about the origin or fate of the universe. Some that are scanning deep space are doing so to find evidence that will confirm or disprove theories about the universe. One such telescope exists to test one of Albert Einstein's most famous theories.

In 1916, in what has been called one of the most brilliant observations of any scientist, physicist Albert Einstein formulated his general theory of relativity, which stands as one of the cornerstones of modern physics. Einstein weaved together space, time, and gravitation, and predicted the existence of such peculiar phenomena as black holes, the expanding universe, and the slowing, stretching, and curving of light as it nears gravitational fields.

The scientific community reveres Einstein as one of the most brilliant physicists since Isaac Newton, yet his general theory of relativity remains one of the least tested of scientific theories. At the beginning of 2004, a team of physicists and astronomers intend to do just that with the assistance of a telescope on the Gravity Probe-B (GP-B) spacecraft.

The purpose of the GP-B telescope, which is unlike any other satellite telescope, is to test two predictions of Einstein's general theory of relativity. It is measuring how space and time are distorted by the presence of the earth's gravitational field and how the earth's rotation spins space and time around with it. On board GP-B are two critical instruments necessary to test these two complicated predictions—a telescope and four gyroscopes. Rex Geveden, the GP-B program manager, announced, "The Gravity Probe B space vehicle houses two of the most challenging science instruments ever devised that seek to answer some of the most important questions about the structure of our universe."[38]

GP-B's telescope is a Cassegrain reflecting telescope with a 5.6-inch mirror made of optically bonded fused quartz. Optical bonding is a method of fusing together quartz parts, without the use of any glue or fasteners, to ensure that the lens does not distort or break when cooled to extremely low temperatures. Unlike most other telescopes, this telescope was not designed to photograph or study fiery objects in deep space; its role was to locate the star HR 8703, named IM Pegasi, known to astronomers as a guide star, and point to it continuously with absolute precision.

The four gyroscopes, perfectly round yet each only the size of a golf ball, spin at ten thousand revolutions per minute. When the experiment began, the telescope established alignment with the guide star and locked on to it without any deviation. The gyroscopes were aligned with the telescope so that initially their spin axes also pointed to the guide star. The gyroscopes were spun, and over the course of a year, while keeping the telescope (and satellite) aligned with the guide star, the gyroscopes' spin axes will be monitored to detect any deflection or drift due to the earth's gravity or spin.

If the predictions based on Einstein's theory are correct, the gyroscopes' spin axes should slowly drift away from their initial guide star alignment—both in the satellite's orbital plane, due to the slowing of time and curving of light, and perpendicular to the orbital plane, due to the earth's spin. Scientific writer Leonard David asserts, "Gravity Probe B is one of the few space missions NASA has conducted with relevance to fundamental physics. If successful, it would assuredly join the ranks of the classical experiments of physics. By the same token, a confirmed result in disagreement with GR [general relativity] would be revolutionary."[39]

Following thirty days of calibration, the mission scientists began to gather data on the precise spin-axis orientation of the gyroscopes. The probe has begun sending back data twice a day. In early 2004, with several months to go, indications are that Einstein's predictions were quite accurate, although NASA expects the final analysis of the huge pile of data to take at least another year.

What questions telescopes will be called upon to answer in the next few decades or next century is nearly impossible to know. Many raised over the past century remain elusive and unanswered, while many more will

Looking Back in Time

Because the universe is so vast, the light and other electromagnetic radiation from faraway stars and galaxies takes millions or even billions of years to reach Earth. This means we are seeing some stars and galaxies as they appeared millions or billions of years ago. As telescopes become more powerful and can see deeper into space, they will also look back farther in time. Future space telescopes may soon be able to observe the universe's first stars.

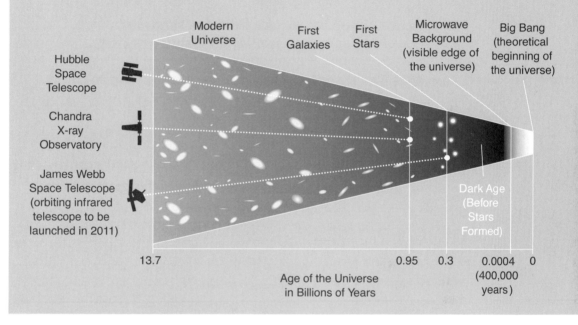

surely be added. Regardless of the number or complexity of telescopes, modern astronomers will continue to indulge their imaginations constructing telescopes that will be just as unbelievable and complicated to present-day telescope builders as the Hubble, Keck, LBT, and GP-B would surely be to Lippershey, Galileo, and Newton. In astronomer Alan Dressler's view:

> Astronomy has given us something that will help answer our ancient questions: Where did we come from? Are we alone in the universe? When the answers to these questions are known, our civilizations will evolve new visions of who we are and what our futures might be. Already we have learned enough to appreciate that the universe is enormous and ancient, but life—tiny and transient —is its precious jewel.[40]

Notes

Introduction: Tools to Answer Cosmic Questions
1. Robert Lin, telephone interview with author, May 20, 2004.

Chapter 1: The First Telescope
2. Quoted in Henry C. King, *The History of the Telescope.* Cambridge, MA: Sky, 1955, p. 37.
3. Quoted in J.J. O'Connor and E.F. Robertson, "Galileo Galilei," School of Mathematical and Computational Sciences, University of St. Andrews, November 2002. www.gap.dcs.st-and.ac.uk.
4. Quoted in King, *The History of the Telescope*, p. 75.

Chapter 2: The Era of the Giants
5. Quoted in King, *The History of the Telescope*, p. 123.
6. Quoted in King, *The History of the Telescope*, p. 123.
7. Quoted in King, *The History of the Telescope*, p. 129.
8. Quoted in Bath Preservation Trust, "William Herschel," 2001. www.bath-preservation-trust.org.uk.
9. Quoted in Bath Preservation Trust, "William Herschel."

Chapter 3: Radio Telescopes: Discovering the Invisible Universe
10. Isaac Asimov, *Eyes on the Universe: A History of Telescopes.* Boston: Houghton Mifflin, 1975, p. 215.
11. Quoted in Wallace H. Tucker and Karen Tucker, *The Cosmic Inquirers: Modern Telescopes and Their Makers.* Cambridge, MA: Harvard University Press, 1986, p. 35.
12. National Radio Astronomy Observatory, "The Very Long Baseline Array," April 2004. www.nrao.edu.
13. Quoted in David Tenenbaum, "Three, Two, One, Contact," The Why Files: Science Behind the News, July 1997. www.why files.org.

Chapter 4: Observing the Violent Universe: X-rays and Gamma Rays

14. Quoted in SpaceRef.Com, "Gamma-ray Bursts, X-ray Flashes, and Certain Supernovae Are Related," November 2003. www.spaceref.com.

15. Tucker and Tucker, *The Cosmic Inquirers*, p. 3.

16. Quoted in Michael Klesius, "Super X-ray Vision," *National Geographic*, December 2002, p. 43.

17. Quoted in Goddard Space Flight Center, "NASA's HETE Spots Rare Gamma-Ray Burst Afterglow," November 7, 2001. www.gsfc.nasa.gov.

18. Quoted in Imagine the Universe! "NASA Detects One of Closest and Brightest Gamma Ray Bursts," May 16, 2003. www.imag ine.gsfc.nasa.gov.

19. Quoted in Spaceflight Now, "Study Reports Origin of Gamma-Ray Bursts," May 17, 2002. www.spaceflightnow.com.

20. Quoted in Imagine the Universe! "Neutron Stars," 2003. www.imagine.gsfc.nasa.gov.

21. Kelly Kizer Whitt, "Record-Setting Gamma-Ray Burst Detected," Astronomy.com, April 2003. www.astronomy.com.

Chapter 5: Hubble

22. Daniel Fisher and Hilmar Duerbeck, *Hubble: A New Window to the Universe*. New York: Springer-Verlag, 1996, p. 26.

23. HubbleSite, "Telescope History: Vision Becomes a Reality," 2003. http://hubblesite.org.

24. Quoted in David Whitehouse, "Hubble's Vision Is Blurred," BBC News, April 2000. www.news.bbc.co.uk.

25. Quoted in Mark Carreau, "Hubble's Eyesight Is 20-20," *San Francisco Chronicle*, January 14, 1994, p. C3.

26. Simon Goodwin, *Hubble's Universe: Portrait of Our Universe*. New York: Penguin, 1997, p. 16.

27. Quoted in Ed Bradley, "Hubble Future in Jeopardy," CBSNews.com, March 14, 2004. www.cbsnews.com.

28. Quoted in Bradley, "Hubble Future in Jeopardy."

29. Quoted in Bradley, "Hubble Future in Jeopardy."

Chapter 6: Peering into the Future

30. Quoted in Laura K. Kraft, "Hubble and Keck Team Up to Find Farthest Known Galaxy," W.M. Keck Observatory, February 2004. www2.keck.hawaii.edu.

31. Richard Wainscoat, "Astronomy and Space Science: Monitoring the Cosmos, Far and Near," State of Hawaii, 1998. www.hawaii.gov.

32. Quoted in W.M. Keck Observatory, "Two Telescopes, One Vision," 2001. www2.keck.hawaii.edu.

33. Ron Hipschman, "SETI: The Radio Search," SETI@home, 2004. www.setiathome.ssl.berkeley.edu.

34. Ron Hipschman, "The Center for SETI Research," SETI Institute, 2003. www.seti-inst.edu.

35. Quoted in Matt Quandt, "GALEX Will Look Ahead to the Past," Astronomy.com, April 2003. www.astronomy.com.

36. Quoted in Quandt, "GALEX Will Look Ahead to the Past."

37. Christopher Martin, telephone interview with author, May 25, 2004.

38. Quoted in Luci Sherriff, "Chocks Away for NASA's Einstein Test," *Register*, April 21, 2004. www.theregister.co.uk.

39. Leonard David, "Gravity Probe B: Delay in Space and Time," Space.com, December 2003. www.space.com.

40. Alan Dressler, "About Origins," Origins, September 2003. www.origins.jpl.nasa.gov.

For Further Reading

Isaac Asimov, *Eyes on the Universe: A History of Telescopes*. Boston: Houghton Mifflin, 1975. Although best known as a science fiction writer, Asimov has written an excellent history of telescopes that traces the development of optical telescopes from Galileo to design considerations for the Hubble Space Telescope. Asimov explains many of the mysteries such as how Newton built the first reflector and how modern cameras allow astronomers to record the heavens and change their ideas about the size, age, and origins of the cosmos.

Daniel Fisher and Hilmar Duerbeck, *Hubble: A New Window to the Universe*. New York: Springer-Verlag, 1996. The first part of this book presents a brief historical overview about astronomy, concentrating on telescopes up to the Hubble project. The central and largest portion discusses the Hubble's operations, as well as future plans for the telescope. The highlight of the book is the 150 color photographs of exotic cosmic forms taken by the Hubble telescope.

Simon Goodwin, *Hubble's Universe: Portrait of Our Universe*. New York: Penguin, 1997. Goodwin provides a short, excellent history about the construction of Hubble, the flawed mirror, and its successful repair. The remainder of the book is composed of a set of fifty full-page superior-quality photographs with accompanying explanations.

Richard Learner, *Astronomy Through the Telescope: The 500 Year Story of the Instruments, the Inventors, and Their Discoveries*. New York: Van Nostrand Reinhold, 1981. This is an excellent history of astronomy for the amateur stargazer. The author traces the history of telescope development and interlaces stories about the men who built and operated them.

W. Patrick McCray, *Giant Telescopes: Astronomical Ambition and the Promise of Technology*. Cambridge, MA: Harvard University Press, 2004. McCray has provided a very readable account of large telescopes in the post–World War II era. He explores large telescope astronomy and America's desire to retain leadership against growing competition from Europe and Japan. The book includes discussions of the major large, modern telescopes and tells the story behind their planning and construction.

Thornton Page and Lou Pace, *Telescopes: How to Make and Use Them*. New York: Macmillan, 1965. This book is a useful primer that explains how several types of telescopes work. The authors describe the components of telescopes and how they are assembled and adjusted for peak performance. Line drawings complement the text.

David O. Woodbury, *The Glass Giant of Palomar*. New York: Dodd, Mead, 1954. This is a great book for astronomy buffs. The author provides a colorful history of the construction of the observatory and the mirror. The book is a lively mix of technical detail and firsthand fascinating stories about the astronomers, workmen, and technicians.

Works Consulted

Books

Martin Cohen, *In Quest of Telescopes*. Cambridge, MA: Sky, 1980. This book describes the travels of the author from observatory to observatory (with accompanying photographs). Cohen visits the largest of the earthbound telescopes, describing their technical attributes and their discoveries.

Nigel Henbest, *Observing the Universe*. Oxford: Blackwell & New Scientist, 1984. This book is filled with explanations, photographs, and maps of the universe. The author provides history about telescopes' discoveries, followed by descriptions of the Milky Way and other neighboring galaxies.

Henry C. King, *The History of the Telescope*. Cambridge, MA: Sky, 1955. The author begins his history of telescopes with ancient Egyptian astronomical instruments and works his way up through the making of the two-hundred-inch Hale telescope at Mt. Palomar, the largest and most innovative at the time his book was published. King includes numerous black-and-white photos and diagrams.

Zdenek Kopal, *Telescopes in Space*. New York: Hart, 1970. The author of this book, a highly regarded astronomer, provides a thorough history of satellite telescopes for their first two decades. The author provides plentiful technical detail and superb photographs.

Staff of the Palomar Observatory, *Giants of Palomar*. Salt Lake City, UT: Hansen Planetarium, 1983. This small booklet, which can be purchased only at the Mt. Palomar Observatory or by mail, provides an excellent short history of the telescope and famous astronomers who have worked there.

Wallace H. Tucker and Karen Tucker, *The Cosmic Inquirers: Modern Telescopes and Their Makers*. Cambridge, MA: Harvard University Press, 1986. The Tuckers provide information on how NASA, Congress, and major universities determine which satellite telescopes will be launched into space. The Tuckers interweave into the fabric of their history fascinating stories about astronomers and the problems they faced.

Periodicals

Mark Carreau, "Hubble's Eyesight Is 20-20," *San Francisco Chronicle*, January 14, 1994.

Chris Carroll, "Eye on Infinity," *National Geographic*, December 2003.

Michael Klesius, "Super X-ray Vision," *National Geographic*, December 2002.

Internet Sources

Bath Preservation Trust, "William Herschel," 2001. www.bath-preserva tion-trust.org.uk.

Ed Bradley, "Hubble Future in Jeopardy," CBSNews.com, March 14, 2004. www.cbsnews.com.

Chandra X-ray Observatory, "Cosmic Look-Back Time," 2004. http:// chandra.harvard.edu.

Leonard David, "Gravity Probe B: Delay in Space and Time," Space.com, December 2003. www.space.com.

Alan Dressler, "About Origins," Origins, September 2003. www.origins. jpl.nasa.gov.

Andrew Fabian, "Black Hole Sound Waves," Science@NASA, September 2003. http://science.nasa.gov.

Goddard Space Flight Center, "NASA's HETE Spots Rare Gamma-Ray Burst Afterglow," November 7, 2001. www.gsfc.nasa.gov.

Ron Hipschman, "SETI: The Radio Search," SETI@home, 2004. www. setiathome.ssl.berkeley.edu.

———, "The Center for SETI Research," SETI Institute, 2003. www.seti-inst.edu.

HubbleSite, "Hubble's Deepest View Ever of the Universe Unveils Earliest Galaxies," May 2003. http://hubblesite.org.

———, "Telescope History: Vision Becomes a Reality," 2003. http://hub blesite.org.

Imagine the Universe! "NASA Detects One of Closest and Brightest Gamma Ray Bursts," May 16, 2003. www.imagine.gsfc.nasa.gov.

———, "Neutron Stars," 2003. www.imagine.gsfc.nasa.gov.

Laura K. Kraft, "Hubble and Keck Team Up to Find Farthest Known Galaxy," W.M. Keck Observatory, February 2004. www2.keck. hawaii.edu.

C.M. Mountain and F.C. Gillett, "The Revolution in Telescope Aperture," AURA: National Optical Astronomy Observatory, 1998. www.aura-nio. noao.edu/documentation/mountain1998.pdf.

Mt. Wilson Observatory, "Adaptive Optics," www.mtwilson.edu.

National Radio Astronomy Observatory, "The Very Long Baseline Array," April 2004. www.nrao.edu.

J.J. O'Connor and E.F. Robertson, "Galileo Galilei," School of Math-ematical and Computational Sciences, University of St. Andrews, November 2002. www.gap.dcs.st-and.ac.uk.

Matt Quandt, "GALEX Will Look Ahead to the Past," Astronomy.com, April 2003. www.astronomy.com.

Luci Sherriff, "Chocks Away for NASA's Einstein Test," *Register*, April 21, 2004. www.theregister.co.uk.

Spaceflight Now, "Study Reports Origin of Gamma-Ray Bursts," May 17, 2002. www.spaceflightnow.com.

SpaceHike.com, "Gamma-Ray Telescope to Sleuth for Origin of Elements," 2003. www.spacehike.com.

SpaceRef.com, "Gamma-ray Bursts, X-ray Flashes, and Certain Supernovae Are Related," November 2003. www.spaceref.com.

David Tenenbaum, "Three, Two, One, Contact," The Why Files: Science Behind the News, July 1997. www.whyfiles.org.

Rob van den Berg, "A Constant That Isn't Constant," *Physical Review Focus*, August 2001. http://focus.aps.org/story/v8/st9.

Richard Wainscoat, "Astronomy and Space Science: Monitoring the Cosmos, Far and Near," State of Hawaii, 1998. www.hawaii.gov.

David Whitehouse, "Hubble's Vision Is Blurred," BBC News, April 2000. www.news.bbc.co.uk.

Kelly Kizer Whitt, "Record-Setting Gamma-Ray Burst Detected," Astronomy.com, April 2003. www.astronomy.com.

W.M. Keck Observatory, "Two Telescopes, One Vision," 2001. www2. keck.hawaii.edu.

Web Sites

Chandra X-ray Observatory (http://chandra.harvard.edu). This site provides information about the Chandra telescope's history, progress, and discoveries. It also contains spectacular photographs and links to all major project objectives.

HubbleSite (http://hubblesite.org). The Hubble site, operated by the Jet Propulsion Laboratory, is an impressive collection of information about the history of Hubble and its remarkable accomplishments. The site includes dazzling photographs, and it welcomes queries about the Hubble telescope from students.

SETI@home (www.setiathome.ssl.berkeley.edu). SETI is a scientific experiment that uses Internet-connected computers in the search for extraterrestrial intelligence. The site provides detailed information about SETI's mission and how anyone with a home computer can participate in the analysis of possible signals from intelligent alien beings.

W.M. Keck Observatory (www2.keck.hawaii.edu). The Keck Observatory Web site offers information on the twin Keck telescopes. Engineering discussions about the ten-meter mirrors, the instrumentation of the telescopes, and the objectives astronomers hope to achieve are included in the site's array of Web pages.

Index

Picture Credits

About the Author

James Barter received his undergraduate degree in history and classics at the University of California at Berkeley. He then went on to graduate studies in ancient history and archaeology at the University of Pennsylvania. A Fulbright scholar at the American Academy in Rome, Mr. Barter worked on archaeological sites in and around the city as well as on sites in the Naples area. Mr. Barter also has worked and traveled extensively in Greece, and he has taught history and Latin in the United States. Mr. Barter resides in Rancho Santa Fe, California, and lectures throughout the San Diego area.